BREAKTHROUGH PARENTING

BREAKTHROUGH PARENTING

by John Maxwell

PUBLISHING
Colorado Springs, Colorado

BREAKTHROUGH PARENTING
Copyright © 1996 by John Maxwell. All rights reserved. International copyright secured.

Library of Congress Cataloging-in-Publication Data
Maxwell, John C., 1947-
    Breakthrough parenting/by John Maxwell.
        p.   cm.
    Includes bibliographical references.
    ISBN 1-56179-469-4
        1. Parenting—religious aspects—Christianity.   2. Family—religious life.   3. Family—United States.
I. Title.
BV4526.2.M336   1996
248.8'45—dc20   96-2304
                                                                                                              CIP

Published by Focus on the Family Publishing, Colorado Springs, CO 80995. Distributed in the U.S.A. and
Canada by Word Books, Dallas, Texas.

Unless otherwise noted, Scripture quotations are from the HOLY BIBLE, NEW INTERNATIONAL
VERSION ®. Copyright © 1973, 1978, 1984 by the International Bible Society. Used by permission of
Zondervan Publishing House. All rights reserved. Quotations identified NASB are from the *New American
Standard Bible,* © 1960, 1963, 1968, 1971, 1973, 1975, and 1977 by The Lockman Foundation. Used by
permission. Quotations labeled *The Message* are from *The Message: The New Testament in Contemporary English,*
by Eugene H. Peterson, © 1993 by NavPress. Used by permission. All rights reserved. Quotations labeled TLB
are from *The Living Bible,* © 1971. Used by permission of Tyndale House Publishers, Inc., Wheaton, IL 60189.
All rights reserved. Quotations labeled KJV are from the King James Version. Quotations labeled CEV are from
The Contemporary English Version, © 1995 by the American Bible Society. Used by permission.

People's names and certain details of the case studies in this book have been changed to protect the privacy of the
individuals involved. However, the facts of what happened and the underlying principles have been conveyed as
accurately as possible.

No part of this publication may be reproduced, stored in a retrieval system, or transmitted in any form or by any
means—electronic, mechanical, photocopy, recording, or otherwise—without prior permission of the publisher.

Editor: Larry K. Weeden
Front cover design: Candi L. Park
Front cover illustration: Seth Larson/John Brewster Creative Services
Front cover photos: Jim Whitmer

Printed in the United States of America

96 97 98 99/10 9 8 7 6 5 4 3 2

to Melvin and Laura Maxwell,
my awesome parents,
who have taught and modeled breakthrough living
with credibility and consistency every day of their lives . . .

to Larry Maxwell and Trish Throckmorton,
my brother and sister,
who, along with me, are recipients of this incredible blessing—
more valuable than worldly riches . . .

to Margaret Maxwell,
my wife and my love,
whose partnership with me has given me the greatest joy in life . . .

to Elizabeth and Joel Porter Maxwell,
our wonderful children,
for whom we have done our best to pass along
the legacy of breakthrough living . . .

to each of you, this book is dedicated.
May all who come behind us find us faithful.

Contents

Introduction

Breakthrough or Breakdown: The Choice Is Clear

When I was a kid growing up in the 1950s, my favorite activity was wrestling. I had seen Gorgeous George and the other wrestlers on television, and I imitated them in our living room. My regular opponent was my brother, Larry. He's two and a half years older than me. He was bigger than me, stronger than me, and the best athlete I knew. He was the captain of every team he played on, and I idolized him.

Our wrestling mat was the throw rug in the living room. Larry and I would push back the overstuffed armchair and move the coffee table against the wall, and we'd have a pretty good arena. We'd face off, each looking for a chance to grab the other and throw him to the floor. The person hitting the floor was usually me, and when I landed, I was reminded that the rug was a lot thinner than a real wrestling mat.

Sometimes when we wrestled, Dad would come home from work and join in the fun. Usually, he acted as our referee since neither of us was a match for him, but sometimes he'd wrestle with us, too. Dad believed life should be fun, and he loved playing with us.

One night when I was about eight years old, Dad saw that I was getting discouraged because Larry was beating me mercilessly. In fact, Larry had won every match he and I had ever fought. But on this particular night, Dad told Larry, "You're not going to wrestle Johnny tonight. I am."

I thought Larry was tough, but Dad was an even greater challenge. He was really big and strong—much bigger than Larry. He and I wrestled for a long time that night, but I put up a good fight. Every time he was about to pin me, I worked my way out of the hold. I wasn't able to beat him, but to my surprise, he wasn't able to pin me, either!

The next night, once again Dad said, "Johnny and I will be wrestling tonight." And once again, Dad didn't pin me.

That went on for seven nights!

By the end of the week, Larry was itching to get in there and wrestle me. He liked to compete as much as I did, and he wanted to be inside the ring, not outside as a spectator. The next night, Dad said, "Okay, Larry. Now it's your turn to wrestle Johnny."

That next wrestling match was one I'll never forget. It seemed as if we wrestled for hours. Every time Larry got close to pinning me, I wriggled out of his hold. He always had more moves than I did, and he tried every one of them that night. He even tried some maneuvers he didn't know he had, but he still couldn't beat me. He never could pin me that night. And he never pinned me again.

That wrestling match happened more than 40 years ago, but I remember it as clearly as if it happened yesterday. It was a turning point in my life because it changed the way I thought about myself. For the first time, I saw myself as being on the same level with my brother. It gave me confidence to try new things, especially in sports. And that confidence has stayed with me to this day.

What I experienced that night was a breakthrough, thanks to my father. He had been wise enough to see that my wrestling matches with Larry were eroding my confidence, so he found a way to break through that problem. And then he created a situation that encouraged me to overcome the problem myself.

PARENTING FOR BREAKTHROUGHS

If you're like most people, when you consider your ability to be a good parent, you never think about creating breakthroughs for your children. You probably don't even associate breakthroughs with parenting. You're more likely to think of them in the context of science or technology.

If you looked in Webster's *New World Dictionary*, that traditional viewpoint would be reinforced by the definition found there:

breakthrough *n* **1** : an act or point of breaking through an obstruction **2** : an offensive thrust that penetrates and carries beyond a defensive line in warfare **3** : a sudden advance, esp. in knowledge or technique [a medical —].

It's easy to recognize breakthroughs in the lives of such historical people as Alexander the Great, who was a successful general at age 18, a king at 20, and a world conqueror by 30. His brilliance in military strategy made him one of the greatest leaders the world has seen.

Artists and craftsmen have also experienced breakthroughs, such as eighteenth-century violin maker Antonio Stradivari, said to be the greatest-ever maker of stringed instruments. Though he had made instruments from the time he was 12 years old, he began modifying his designs in his forties, and he experienced an incredible breakthrough. The violins he made between the ages of 55 and 75 are considered to be the finest ever produced. Despite all the scientific advances made since the early 1700s, no instrument maker has been able to match the quality of his work.

And who doesn't associate breakthroughs with Albert Einstein, possibly the greatest thinker of the twentieth century? By age 16, he had already begun to articulate some of the ideas for his special theory of relativity. His breakthrough thinking is so radical that it changed the entire scientific community's understanding of space and time.

But you don't have to be an Einstein to experience breakthroughs or to help your children do so. Let me give you a new definition of *breakthrough*, one we can apply to our children whether they're infants, teenagers, or somewhere in between:

breakthrough *n* **1** : a significant advance or change in direction that propels a child closer to his or her potential; the event can be sudden, but it usually comes as the result of ongoing stimulation from a parent or concerned adult; the results are long-lasting and life-changing.

Think of our children's lives as a journey on a road with many forks and obstacles. The day they are born, they start their long trip, and their intended destination is the realization of their God-given potential.

For some children, the journey is rocky. They're unsure of which way to go. They take wrong turns and travel a long way in a wrong direction. Or they can't overcome the obstacles they encounter. They're stopped dead in their tracks, and they never seem to regain the momentum they need to reach their potential.

But for other children, the journey seems easier. They know early on where they're supposed to go, and life's obstacles are of no more concern to them than hurdles are for an Olympic champion.

What makes the second group of children different from the first? Breakthroughs. When children experience breakthroughs, they're able to move further down the road toward the fulfillment of their potential. Sometimes, the breakthrough enables them to choose the better fork in the road. Other times, the breakthrough allows them to overcome an obstacle or potential obstacle with relative ease, and it gives them an extra burst of energy that speeds them on their journey.

> **When children experience breakthroughs, they're able to move further down the road toward the fulfillment of their potential.**

In the case of me and the wrestling match, my father had seen a potential obstacle in the road of my journey—discouragement and lessened self-worth. And he created a circumstance that allowed me to break through that obstacle by increasing my confidence. He didn't *remove* the obstacle by stopping us from wrestling or telling Larry to let me win. And he didn't *leave me alone* to work it out entirely for myself, figuring that someday when I was older, I would win. He *created the opportunity* for a breakthrough, and then he *encouraged me* as I experienced it for myself.

A SERIES OF BREAKTHROUGHS

During my life, I've experienced a series of breakthroughs, beginning with many that came as the result of my upbringing. My parents modeled break-through living, and they taught it to me. Sometimes the breakthroughs were carefully planned, as was the case in the revolutionary allowance system my father developed for my brother, sister, and me (see breakthrough #6), and in his approach to our education (see breakthrough #4).

Other times, my parents recognized critical moments in our lives, and they seized those moments to help us experience a breakthrough (see break-through #1). That was the case in an incident that occurred when I was a senior in college. I was preparing to graduate at 22 years old, and I was one of the candidates for an award to be given to the Most Promising Student. As it turned out, another student and I finished in a tie. My father, who was the college president, had the responsibility of breaking the tie and decid-ing who would get the award.

My father could have handled the situation in several ways. He could have picked me to get the award because I was his son and then justified it in some way. Or he could have picked the other boy to show impartiality and never let me know there had been a tie. But instead, he picked a path that bene-fited me *and* the other student, helping both of us experience breakthroughs. He took me aside prior to graduation and said, "John, I want you to know that you and another boy have tied for this award. But I can't give it to you. I know you will be successful in your life, and this award isn't necessary for you to achieve that success. But it will mean a lot to the other boy. It will really help him on his way."

That comment from my dad made a big impact on me. It sharpened my already developing sense of destiny. And it also showed me Dad's deep respect for me and his belief that God would use me in a special way. It was an important breakthrough in my life.

PARENTS LEAD . . . CHILDREN FOLLOW

Children rarely experience breakthroughs on their own. Left alone, few will travel quickly down the road to their potential. They need their parents to help them along. But to help children experience a breakthrough, parents first need to experience their own. You can't give what you don't have.

We must first make a breakthrough in the way we think about parenting. We need to recognize our ability to create life-changing breakthroughs in our children's lives. We can help them overcome the obstacles most people face. The burst of energy that results will give them an extra push and greater momentum so they can reach their potential. No matter whether your children are in preschool or high school, they can use a boost and assistance in overcoming obstacles.

BARRIERS TO BREAKTHROUGH

Most children aren't enjoying breakthroughs, however, because their parents haven't yet experienced their own breakthrough in the way they approach parenting. There are barriers to that breakthrough, but they can be overcome. Here are five of the most common:

1. Instead of trying to create breakthroughs, we react according to old patterns. Most of us raise our kids in a way very similar to the way our parents raised us. If our parents didn't cultivate breakthroughs in our lives, we probably won't be on the lookout for opportunities to do it for our children. But the good news is that we can change the pattern—if we're willing to work at it. Recognize that creating breakthroughs is an essential part of parenting.

2. We don't try something innovative or creative because it goes against conventional thinking. We all begin the parenting process with little experience, so we learn as we go along. Usually, new parents look to trusted friends and family members for advice. They get an idea of what most people do and then do something similar.

But that approach doesn't always produce the best results. At times, another person's methods won't work for you, or the best course of action may be to go against conventional wisdom. And if you're trying to break away from negative patterns that developed in your family of origin, advice from family members won't help. They're likely to suggest that you do what they did, which will only lead you to repeat their mistakes.

3. We're limited by the belief that our children won't respond positively. Being a parent is wonderful, but it can also cause a person to get into a rut. A mother who has told her toddler not to play with his food a dozen times in the last 10 minutes—and whose child is still playing with his peas—may believe at that moment that her child will never listen to her, and she may not even want to attempt a breakthrough. But sometimes a great opportunity comes at just such a moment.

As parents, we can't afford to give up or become pessimistic. When we see an opportunity to create a breakthrough, we need to seize it, believing our children can and will respond positively. They may not do it every time, but it takes only a few breakthroughs to change a life in a positive way.

4. We desire perfection. Many times when we teach our children, we unrealistically expect them to respond perfectly to our instruction. We show them how to wash the car, and we expect them to do it right every time thereafter. We show them how to wash the dishes once, and we expect them never to do a sloppy job again. But that's not how it is in real life. No matter how well we teach, they will respond imperfectly because they're not perfect.

Constantly pointing out to our children what they're doing wrong will discourage them from trying, and that discouragement will become an obstacle. Instead, we must learn to have realistic expectations and accept their best effort even when it's not perfect. And that includes not getting upset when they fail to respond positively to our breakthrough attempts.

5. When we try a breakthrough idea and don't see immediate results, we want to give up. Even if our children respond positively to our efforts, we may have to wait a long time before we see results. That can be discouraging. But creating breakthroughs in a child's life is a lengthy process. It's like growing a giant redwood. Even when a young plant breaks through the surface of the soil, it has only just begun the growing process. Years will go by as it gets bigger and stronger. Its roots will have to break through successive layers of soil during its lifetime. It will have to compete with other trees for nutrients and space. It may have to survive a fire or two. And it will have to grow very tall among its fellow redwoods before its branches reach up into the sunlight. But eventually, as all those individual breakthroughs build upon each other, the redwood will become a strong, mature tree.

WHEN CAN WE EXPERIENCE A BREAKTHROUGH?

How do moms and dads break through the obstacles and begin to help their children? Three conditions (for children as well as the parents) make a person ready for a breakthrough.

1. When We Feel the Heat

Whenever a person is feeling the heat—emotionally, physically, or spiritually—it creates a climate for growth. Pain prompts change. So the good news is that *if you're having a hard time with one of your children, you're a candidate for a breakthrough*. It's like the Chinese symbol for the word *crisis:* It means "danger," but it also means "opportunity." There's a possibility hidden in every problem.

Not long ago, I did a study on miracles in the Bible, and I discovered they all had one thing in common. Every single one was preceded by a problem. Isn't that amazing? Without problems, there can be no miracles. Now, that doesn't mean every problem we face will result in a miracle. Nor does it mean every difficulty will result in a breakthrough. But it does mean one thing: If you're feeling the heat, you're ripe for a miracle.

The first step in the process is to acknowledge the problem. The people who came to Jesus for a miracle admitted something was wrong. If that's your situation now, that's where you need to begin. If you're not facing up to the problem, you won't be able to experience a positive solution or breakthrough.

> Without problems, there can be no miracles.

The next step is to try to look at problems as

opportunities—for growth, for a change in direction, for hidden possibilities. That's not easy, but it is necessary. When times are really tough and you're hurting, think about Jesus. Every trouble He experienced ended in triumph.

2. When We See the Light

People are also prepared to make a breakthrough when they can see positive possibilities in the light of change. As I tell people in conferences, if you always do what you've always done, you'll always get what you've always gotten. But when you learn new methods and try them, you open the door for a breakthrough.

Parents who grew up with poor role models or unhealthy home situations have the greatest need to learn new skills, but they also have the greatest potential for positive change. One key to tap in to that potential is to use creativity. It takes a lot of creativity to deal with reality. Creative people can overcome obstacles that others can't. Anna Freud said, "Creative minds always have been known to survive any kind of bad training."

In his book *A Whack on the Side of the Head*, Roger von Oech identified several barriers to creative thinking. They're summarized in the following 10 phrases on the left.[1] On the right are 10 phrases I use to counteract them:

1. That's not logical.	*1. Listen to your intuition.*
2. Follow the rules.	*2. Think results.*
3. Be practical.	*3. Be outrageous.*
4. To err is wrong.	*4. To err and learn from the mistake is to be one step closer to a breakthrough.*
5. There's one right answer.	*5. The possibilities are endless.*
6. Play is frivolous.	*6. Play is refreshing.*
7. Avoid ambiguity.	*7. Explore ambiguity.*
8. That's not my area.	*8. Be a no-limit thinker.*
9. Don't be foolish.	*9. Take a leap of faith.*
10. I'm not creative.	*10. I am creative—I was formed in God's image!*

I want to help you see the light. One of my goals in writing this book is to present some of the methods and ideas my parents used with me. They're proven and successful. Not all of what my parents did may be right for you; not all of it was right for me. But if you can develop a breakthrough mind-set for parenting or receive just one breakthrough idea that you can use, I will consider this effort to be a success. This book may be just the beginning, because one idea sparks another, and one breakthrough inevitably leads to another.

3. When We Receive the Strength

Finally, people become capable of a breakthrough when they receive enough strength to make one. That strengthening can come from a number of things:

1. Permission. I see people all the time who seem to be waiting for permission to be successful. They hang back, waiting for a promotion. Or they dream about starting their own business—but they keep waiting, hoping someone will tell them it's time to get started. Many parents act the same way. They're hoping someone will give them permission to break through and do something new and exciting with their children.

That need for permission reminds me of a time when my wife, Margaret, and I were out for a drive in southern Ohio, and we were getting thirsty. We stopped at a fast-food place, and when I tried to order a diet soft drink for Margaret, we discovered they didn't sell any. (This was quite a few years ago.) I thought, *No sweat. I'll just get her a cup of ice and pick up a canned diet drink along the way*. But when I ordered the ice, the girl behind the counter said uncertainly, "I don't think I can do that."

"Sure you can," I said with a smile. She paused for a moment, not knowing what to do, and then suddenly she returned the smile and said, "Okay, let me get it for you." All she needed was someone to give her permission.

Please give me the privilege of saying to you, yes, you can! You have permission to become the parent God created you to be. You can do it! You can help your children break through many of the barriers to fulfilling their potential that they'll face.

Now, that doesn't mean you'll suddenly become the perfect parent. But it does mean you can become a *better* parent. And you've got a shot at becoming the kind of parent who cultivates breakthroughs in your children's lives. Just don't be too afraid of making mistakes. You're going to make some whether you try for a breakthrough or not, so why not shoot for the stars?

2. Freedom. A friend named Fred Rowe is a psychiatrist whose specialty is children and adolescents. According to the standards in our society, he's an expert in raising children. But Fred is also the father of three small boys, and he once told me, "There are no experts when it comes to parenting. And the people who tell you they *are* experts are not telling you the truth."

Let me share a secret with you: When you don't feel obligated to listen to the experts, it gives you a lot of freedom. It multiplies the possibilities, and it increases your creativity. It helps you see old things in new ways.

That reminds me of the story I once heard about F. W. Woolworth. When he opened his first store, a merchant down the street ran an ad in the local paper that said, "Do your local shopping here. We've been in business for 50 years!"

Woolworth immediately ran an ad of his own in response. It read, "We've been in business only one week. All our merchandise is brand-new!"

As Asian scholar Shunryu Suzuki said, "In the beginner's mind there are many possibilities; in the expert's mind there are few." To have the best chance of making breakthroughs in parenting, bring a fresh outlook to your parenting every day.

After quoting my friend Fred Rowe, I'm smart enough not to claim to be an expert on parenting, either. I'm just a parent like you, doing the best I can and praying that my kids, Elizabeth (19 at the time of this writing) and Joel Porter (17), turn out to be adults who love and serve God. But I was fortunate to have creative and supportive parents. They did many wonderful things with me and my siblings to help us reach our potential, and I'm sharing their methods and results with you.

The bottom line is that the only real expert on parenting is God. All other sources are merely stating opinion. As parents, if we stay within the guidelines laid down in Scripture, we have the freedom to be as creative and innovative as we can be. That's what my parents did, and that's what I recommend to you.

3. Self-confidence. In *A Whack on the Side of the Head,* Roger von Oech made an insightful comment about breakthroughs that relates to confidence. He said, "Almost every advance in art, cooking, medicine, agriculture, engineering, marketing, politics, education, and design has occurred when someone challenged the rules and tried another approach."[2]

Trying a new approach in any area takes confidence, but trying to be innovative in parenting can be especially intimidating. However, you can find confidence in the knowledge that God has called you to this task. Ephesians 6:4 says, "Parents, don't be hard on your children. Raise them properly. Teach them and instruct them about the Lord" (CEV). God has called us to raise our children, and we can be confident He would not ask of us anything we are unable to do.

4. A sense of humor. It's impossible to overestimate the importance of a sense of humor when it comes to being a parent. But if you have children, you probably already knew that. Someone once said, "God gave us imagination to make up for what we aren't, and a sense of humor to console us for what we are."

I encourage you to bring a sense of humor to everything you do as a parent. Some of my fondest memories are of the fun times I had with my folks. For example, when we went grocery shopping with my dad—and he always did it so Mom wouldn't have to—he used to go down the aisles picking the things we needed. But instead of placing them in the basket, he would toss them up in the air over his shoulder. It was Larry's and my job to catch the boxes and cans and put them in the basket. No wonder we turned out to be good athletes!

I remember one time in the store in Circleville, Ohio, when Dad was doing his usual thing, tossing boxes of cereal, canned beans, onions—you name it. Then he launched a can of corn a little harder than he should have. Larry scrambled for it, but it went over his head and into the next aisle, where we heard a tremendous crash. Dad had taken out a whole row of catsup bottles. We didn't know what Dad would do, but he just laughed. And, of course, he paid the grocer for the catsup.

Mom had a great sense of humor, too. I remember one time when Larry was six and I was about four, and we'd gotten into trouble for going someplace we weren't supposed to go. Mom was getting ready to spank us, which she used to do with a kitchen spatula. Since Larry was older, she knew he was the ringleader, and he was going to get his spanking first.

There we were in the kitchen, waiting for our punishment. Larry bent over, and when Mom gave his bottom a smack, we heard a loud *bang*. Smoke began to rise from Larry's pants. At first, both Larry and Mom looked shocked. I thought she had killed him. But then Mom started laughing, and so did we. You see, Larry had put a bunch of caps in his back pockets, and when Mom spanked him, they went off. When Mom saw his bottom smoldering, she couldn't contain her laughter. And I thought it was great because I didn't get spanked that day.

5. God's assistance. Finally, the ultimate strengthening a person can receive is assistance from God. Scripture tells us that without God, we can do nothing, but that with Him, all things are possible (see John 15:5 and Luke 1:37). So you probably agree that it's important for God to be involved if a life-changing breakthrough is to occur. But you may wonder, How do I ask God to help me?

I recommend that you start by praying for wisdom. James 1:5 states, "If any of you lacks wisdom, he should ask God, who gives generously to all without finding fault, and it will be given to him." No matter what your circumstances, you can gain wisdom. If you're just getting started as a parent, now is a good time to ask God for help. If you've been a parent for a while and you've already had problems, made major mistakes, and hurt your children, you can still become a better parent. Even if those early, impressionable years of your children have passed, it's not too late. You can still help them experience breakthroughs.

Second, I suggest you ask God to give you the desire and strength to change. As parents, we're more likely to ask God to change our children than us. But the truth is that we won't be able to change them if we don't first make the necessary changes in ourselves.

Any one of these five components—permission, freedom, self-confidence, a sense of humor, and God's assistance—can be enough to help you experience a breakthrough. If you have more than one in your life, the opportunities increase. And if you have all five, there's no telling what can happen!

Breakthroughs are like stepping-stones in a person's life. Each time you experience one, you have a better chance of experiencing another. But it's also true that if you aren't moving forward toward your potential, you're probably moving in the opposite direction—and that can lead to a breakdown. In life, *if you're not moving in the direction of your God-given potential, you're headed the wrong way.*

As I close this introduction, I hope you can begin to see the incredible power a breakthrough can create in a person's life. And I hope you now realize that breakthroughs aren't just for people who are lucky, brilliant, talented, or rich. Everyone can experience breakthroughs. In writing this book, I hope to help you change your thinking a little and to give you ideas. Maybe you'll use one or more of the breakthrough principles discussed in the following chapters. Or maybe they'll help you come up with ideas of your own. Either way, I know you can do it!

I'm also stopping to say a prayer for you right now—a scriptural prayer. But before I do, let me teach you how to pray Scripture. It's one of the best things I did for the people in my congregation when I was a pastor. Here's how to do it: Begin by selecting a passage from the Bible. You'll want to pick one that speaks to your heart on the subject you'll be praying about. (Paul's letters are especially good for this, and so are any of the promises God made throughout Scripture.) Read the passage, applying what the Scripture says to you or another person. People receive special blessings when they pray God's will and promises back to Him.

The passage I'm praying for you is Hebrews 13:20-21:

> May the God of peace, who through the blood of the eternal covenant brought back from the dead our Lord Jesus, that great Shepherd of the sheep, equip you with everything good for doing his will, and may he work in us what is pleasing to him, through Jesus Christ, to whom be glory for ever and ever. Amen.

And here's my prayer for you:

> Heavenly Father, You are *the God of peace.* It is *through the blood of the eternal covenant* that You *brought back from the dead our Lord*

Jesus. And that same power is still at work in the life of every believer. Lord, I ask that You bless the parents and future parents who are reading this book. You are the *great Shepherd,* and we're Your *sheep.* I ask that You *equip* these parents *with everything good for doing* Your *will.* I ask that You empower them, by Your Holy Spirit, to be the parents You created them to be. I ask, Lord, that they would experience positive change in their lives, and that their children would receive the benefits of those changes so that those kids would experience breakthroughs only You can author. My hope and prayer are that You *may work in us what is pleasing to You, through Jesus Christ, to whom be glory for ever and ever.* Thank You in advance for Your incredible blessings. *Amen.*

Breakthrough #1

See Your Child
Not as He Is,
But as He Could Be

The potential breakthrough for the parent . . .
hope

The potential breakthrough for the child . . .
the ability to reach his or her potential

Some of the happiest times for parents are the days following the birth of a child. Just visit the nursery in any hospital maternity ward. You'll see that it's a place of joy and celebration. Margaret and I were typical parents in that respect. When we first saw our children, we were filled with happiness and anticipation. But we were also different from most parents because our joy came at home. You see, we adopted both of our children.

In the case of Elizabeth, we had a long wait before she came to us. We had expected to get her when she was seven months old, but we had to wait four long months for her. By the time she came to us, she was nearly a year old and could already walk.

But our delight was undiminished. On December 2, 1977, the social worker brought Elizabeth home to us. About a week before, they had told us she was finally coming, and we were so excited. I could hardly sleep, because those months of waiting had almost killed me. Mom and Dad were with us when the social worker arrived. She came in and set Elizabeth down in our living room. Elizabeth had never seen us before, but when Margaret held out her arms and called to her, tiny Elizabeth ran unsteadily to her and was engulfed in a tremendous hug. She was the most loving child—and still is.

There are good reasons we're so ecstatic when a baby arrives. Certainly, there's the celebration of new life. There's also joy in watching a child learn and grow. But we get excited because each baby is a bundle of undeveloped, incredible potential. In our arms may be a doctor who will heal the sick, an evangelist, a president of the United States, or a missionary who will travel the backwaters of a distant nation proclaiming the name of Jesus. Our hope is off the charts because the possibilities seem endless.

But rarely does our hope stay at that high level. Something happens between the maternity ward and junior high school. By the time our kids reach their teens, the hopes and expectations of most of us have eroded. We've had to live with them day in and day out, through the bad as well as the good. And we've seen them for who they really are—depraved human beings, just like us. So how do we move beyond our disappointments and recapture the dreams for our children? We do it by remembering the potential we once recognized in them when they were babies.

THE POWER OF POTENTIAL

Every person God created has nearly limitless potential. It's one of God's gifts to us. What we do with it is our gift to God. So no matter where your children are—newborn infants lying in their cribs, straight-A students getting ready to go off to college, or gang members serving time in juvenile detention—they all have room to improve and have potential they haven't even touched.

A couple of years ago, I cut out a statement about potential that really struck me. It said:

> From the day we were born, we should have been taught about our uniqueness as individuals. We should have learned about the spark of divinity instilled in each of us at birth. Science recognizes only two infinities—outer space, and inner space—the human mind. This three pound mass of cells can store up to one hundred trillion bits of information. When necessary, it can handle up to fifteen thousand decisions per second, as in the case of the digestive process following eating.
>
> Our sense of touch can detect a projection only one twenty-five thousandth of an inch high. We can taste one part quinine in two million parts water. We can smell up to ten thousand different odors. Our body produces every chemical needed to heal itself. Each of us is literally a mass of positive potential.

And that description focuses only on our minds and bodies. It doesn't take into account the potential of the immortal souls God has given us!

Unlock and Open the Door to Potential

As parents, we should work to unlock our children's potential. In the end, that's the greatest gift we can give them—to help them become the people God created them to be. When they don't develop toward their potential, it's a tragedy. Oliver Wendell Holmes once said that failure to fully utilize our abilities is the great tragedy in America. And Harvard theologian Harvey Cox stated it even more strongly: "Shirking responsibility for the full actualization of human potential is the greatest sin of humankind."

Keep in mind, however, that we're not responsible for our children *reaching* their potential. Ultimately, they make the decisions that determine their destiny. But God calls us to unlock our own potential and to help others do the same. And in the case of our children, that means encouraging them and moving them in the right direction. (Breakthrough #2 will discuss ways of discovering what that direction is.)

Reaching Potential Is Biblical

Look at some of the Scriptures that encourage us to reach our potential. In 1 Corinthians 9:24, Paul told us to strive for our potential as a runner would: "Do you not know that those who run in a race all run, but only one receives the prize? *Run in such a way that you may win*" (NASB, emphasis added). In 1 Thessalonians 4:1, we're encouraged to excel still more in the way we live. And 2 Corinthians 13:11 urges, "Be made complete" (NASB) or "Aim for perfection."

Jesus is our model for encouraging others to reach their potential. For example, when the rich young ruler approached Jesus, Scripture says Jesus looked at him and loved him. Then He told the man how he could reach his potential: by selling everything, giving to the poor, and following Him (see Mark 10:17-23). Unfortunately, the young man turned away from his potential—at least on that day.

We can also see Jesus' desire to encourage people in His interaction with

Simon Peter. Ralph G. Turnbull said, "Many probably saw the sand-like nature in Simon—wavering, shifting, fluctuating—but the Son of Man saw his rock-like character and gave him the name Peter. Christ saw gems where others saw only pebbles."

When Jesus nicknamed Simon "Rocky," He was aware that His disciple would deny Him three times. But Jesus looked beyond that and encouraged Peter to reach his potential anyway.

Every Child Is a Rocky

Like Peter, our children have tremendous potential, and at the same time they will almost certainly fail. The important thing is that we focus on their potential, not on their failure to reach it! Sometimes that isn't easy, especially when we're surrounded by problems. On those tough days as parents, we're a little like the mother of three rambunctious children. When they asked her what she wanted for her birthday, she said, "I would like three well-behaved children."

One of her kids then exclaimed, "Oh, boy! Then there'll be six of us!"

Margaret and I sometimes have tough days with our strong-willed son, Joel Porter. But we have a saying that helps us keep our perspective and focus on his potential. When one of us is ready to kill him, the other says, "Be nice to him, Honey, and someday he'll invite you to the White House."

> Our children have tremendous potential, and at the same time they will almost certainly fail.

OVERCOME POTENTIAL OBSTACLES

The majority of people fail to reach their potential—most don't even come close. One reason is that they never overcome the common obstacles to potential, most of which are internal rather than external, contrary to what many people think. Nearly all the obstacles relate to the way people think—to attitudes. Here are five guidelines that will help you overcome the most common obstacles to potential:

Don't Let Your Current Environment Discourage You

A mother of four notoriously unruly children was once asked whether she would have children again if she had it to do over. Sure, she replied, but not the same ones! Maybe that's the way you're feeling right now. You love your children, and you want to help them reach their potential, but things may seem pretty hopeless at the moment.

I'm reminded of a story I heard about Robert Moffat, the missionary. After years of service in South Africa, Moffat returned to Scotland to recruit workers. One cold winter night, he was scheduled to speak at a church, and he was unhappy when he found only a small group of women in attendance because he had geared his message especially to men. Its text was Proverbs 8:4: "Unto you, O men, I call" (KJV).

Moffat felt discouraged, and though he thought his effort would go unrewarded, he preached his message anyway, without a man in the house. But up in the choir loft, unseen by Moffat, was a small boy who was there to pump the organ bellows. That boy listened intently to Moffat and was deeply challenged. He promised God he would follow in the missionary's footsteps.

When that young boy grew up, he went to Africa and became one of the world's most famous missionaries. His name was David Livingstone.

If your present environment isn't what you'd like it to be, don't despair. Try to focus on what's positive, and remember that no matter how bleak things seem, God can help you. In Psalm 121:1-2, the psalmist declared, "I lift up my eyes to the hills—where does my help come from? My help comes from the LORD, the Maker of heaven and earth." Hang in there and rely on God. The work you do today to help your child reach his or her potential will have rewards in the future, even if you can't see them.

Face Your Fears

Fear is a powerful enemy of potential. It robs people of initiative and the willingness to take risks. It impedes their change and growth. It strangles their dreams. As Norman Cousins said, "People are never more insecure than when they become obsessed with their fears at the expense of their dreams."

Most people hindered by fear are afraid of failing. They consider failure to be final or fatal. But their problems don't ultimately defeat them; their *thinking* about their problems does them in. In *The Screwtape Letters*, C. S. Lewis wrote that Satan's strategy is to make Christians preoccupied with their failures because when that happens, the enemy has already won the battle.

The truth is that all successful people fail, and the road to your potential will be paved with failures you experience along the way. Proverbs 24:16 states, "Though a righteous man falls seven times, he rises again." Successful people always get up one more time than they fall down.

We have to face fear our whole lives as parents. We worry when our children take their first wobbly steps, and our fear never really goes away. Margaret and I recently sent Elizabeth off to college, and we still worry about her. But we can't allow our fears to rule our actions. We could keep Elizabeth home with us forever to calm our fears, but that would create a huge obstacle to her potential. Instead, we had to face our fears and let her go.

If fear is preventing you and your children from reaching your potential, you need to face your fears. You may feel overwhelmed or paralyzed. If you do, get some help. Talk to your pastor or a professional Christian counselor. If your fear is of the usual variety—and we *all* experience fear—one of the best ways to learn to overcome it is to get a few wins under your belt. Once you realize that fear can be conquered, you'll be more likely to take risks and keep growing. And the same is true for your children. Once they taste a few victories, they're more likely to face their fears and overcome them.

For example, when Elizabeth was in elementary school, she was asked to sell candy to raise money. The whole idea was traumatic for her because she was pretty shy and she didn't like talking to strangers, much less asking them for money. I knew she would need a little help and a few victories to help her along. I started by helping her decide what she would say, and then I picked out several friends who I knew would buy candy from her. We drove from one friend's house to another, and at each stop she made a sale. Before long, she had sold her first box of candy bars.

By then I thought Elizabeth had experienced enough wins to move on to the next phase: selling to strangers. We drove to another neighborhood, and I waited on the sidewalk while she went up to each door and made her pitch.

I told her to expect to make a sale at one house out of four, so when she did even better, she really felt like a winner. By the time she had finished selling the second box, she didn't want to stop. "Let me sell some more. Okay, Dad?" she asked.

"You'd better believe it," I told her, and off we went. This time, though, I parked the car and waited while she went from door to door on that block. She was working without a safety net. I might have gotten worried about her since she was working alone, but I didn't. The wins she had under her belt helped both of us have confidence.

Don't Always Expect the Experts to Be Right

You've already seen that I'm sometimes skeptical when it comes to experts. I know that just because people are in positions of authority, that doesn't necessarily mean they have all the answers. Consider these opinions once given by experts:

- Beethoven's music teacher said about him, "As a composer he is hopeless."
- When Thomas Edison was a young boy, his teachers said he was so stupid that he could never learn anything.
- When F. W. Woolworth was 21, he got a job in a store but was not allowed to wait on customers because he "didn't have enough sense."
- Walt Disney was once fired by a newspaper editor because he was thought to have "no good ideas."
- World-famous tenor Enrico Caruso was told by one music teacher, "You can't sing. You have no voice at all."
- Louisa Mae Alcott, author of *Little Women*, was told by an editor that she was incapable of writing anything that would have popular appeal.[1]

Just because people have experience or talent in an area doesn't necessarily mean they can see potential in others. I remember that when I was in fifth grade, I wanted to learn to play the trumpet, and I was really excited about it. But when I met with the band teacher, he said, "You can never be a good trumpet player. Your bite is all wrong. You should try another instrument."

My parents, not knowing better, switched me to the clarinet. I played it halfheartedly for a while and then gave it up. I had really wanted to play the trumpet. I've often wondered what would have happened if I had been allowed to continue with it despite the "expert's" opinion.

If your children are excited about learning and want to try something new, encourage them. And think twice before you accept any expert's negative advice. That person's opinion may be a roadblock to their potential. If what your kids want to do is morally wrong or harmful to them, don't allow it. But otherwise, help them along.

Don't Take Shortcuts

I learned one of the most important lessons of my life as a child. Dad always used to say, "You can play now and pay later. Or you can pay now and play later." It's true in nearly every aspect of life. For anything you gain, you pay some kind of price. You can pay it on the front end, or you can pay it on the back end, but either way, you'll pay. For example, if you've done any kind of financial investing, you probably know this is true. If you start making financial sacrifices in your twenties or thirties to build a retirement account, you can play later in life. But if you play now by spending everything you make, you'll pay later by having a more difficult

> # God honors and celebrates the small steps we take as long as they're steps in the right direction.

time financially in your golden years.

That's one reason we should never take shortcuts. They never pay off in the long run. They rob us of experience, gratitude, maturation, and discipline, and they also get us into the habit of relying on ourselves instead of God. Besides, in the end we'll pay for them, and when we pay on the back end, we usually pay more.

God honors and celebrates the small steps we take as long as they're steps in the right direction. When Zerubbabel began the work of rebuilding the Lord's temple in Jerusalem, for example, even though he started slowly, the

Bible says God was pleased: "Do not despise this small beginning, for the eyes of the Lord rejoice to see the work begin, to see the plumbline in the hand of Zerubbabel" (Zech. 4:10, TLB).

Whenever your children begin a new venture, do what you can to get them started right. Teach them to avoid shortcuts. Show them that paying on the front end pays off in the long run. Life is a marathon, and you want them to make it to the finish line.

Choose Your Friends Wisely

Most parents agree that who their children choose as friends makes a difference in their development. It's a cliché, but birds of a feather really do flock together. If your children spend most of their time with kids from worldly families, they will probably be influenced strongly in that direction. As Paul said in 1 Corinthians 15:33, "Do not be misled: 'Bad company corrupts good character.'"

But we parents rarely consider that the people *we* choose as our own friends also affect our children's development in two ways:

1. The children of our friends will likely become the friends of our children.
2. The people we associate with strongly influence who we will become.

We almost never rise above the level of our closest friendships. If those friends are negative, we will likely become negative. If they aren't growing, we probably won't be growing, either. And if we're not modeling growth and development to our children, they probably won't grow toward their potential as they could.

FOCUS ON POTENTIAL

Becoming parents who see children not as they are but as they could be takes time and deliberate effort. It doesn't happen overnight, but it really pays off. The key is to focus on our children's potential.

My parents constantly encouraged us and helped us recognize our potential. I believe that Larry, Trish, and I would not be experiencing life with the degree of fullness we currently enjoy if it weren't for our parents' assistance in this area. They followed five principles that you can also use to develop the right focus:

Develop a Potential Mind-Set

Our ability to develop other people's potential depends on the way we think. We see things not as *they* are, but as *we* are. If we have the mind-set that everything around us has potential, including ourselves, we're likely to see potential in our children. But if our attitudes are poor and we tend to be pessimistic, we probably won't have much hope for our children. God didn't create us to fail in reaching our potential. He created us to win the race. We should heed these words: "He who began a good work in you will carry it on to completion" (Phil. 1:6).

Begin today. Start by thinking about your potential. Better yet, rate yourself. On a scale of 1 to 10 (with perfection being a 10), what is your potential?

Write that number here: _____.

No matter what number you wrote, I guarantee you're not currently reaching it. In fact, if you're like most people, the number you wrote is lower than your real potential.

So what can you do to reach your potential? Begin exploring the possibilities. Look at each day as an opportunity to move one step closer to your potential. Create a plan to grow yourself. Then begin to look at others in terms of their potential. Any time you see a chance to assist others in their growth, help them along. The more potential you see every day for yourself and others, the more you'll be able to help your children reach their potential. Neither you nor I nor our children can be all God intends for us to be until we begin to focus on what we can become.

Model Growth as a Parent

Nothing is better for encouraging children to reach their potential than positive growth modeled by their parents. People do what they see, and that's especially true for children. When our kids are young, they'll do what we say regardless of what we do. But by the time they reach their early teens, they begin doing what we *do* even when it differs from what we *say*.

Parents who are continually working to develop their own potential mentally, spiritually, emotionally, and physically have children who will see that process as normal. Parents who aren't growing won't be able to guide their children's growth effectively. They can't lead their kids down a path they've never traveled.

When it comes to personal growth, most people fall into one of three zones:

1. The coasting zone: The person in the coasting zone often focuses on what he has done in the past because he's not doing much in the present. For him, life is a series of bare-minimum days. This person keeps a low profile. And if it's possible to do less today than yesterday, the person in the coasting zone will do exactly that. He doesn't want to hear about his potential.

2. The comfort zone: The person in the comfort zone may work hard but may never grow. She sticks with what she knows because it's safe. She may acknowledge that growth is a good thing, but she's not willing to pay the price to grow herself. As a result, she'll never reach her potential.

3. The challenge zone: The person who lives in the challenge zone is constantly striving to reach his potential. He's not content to live on yesterday's victories. Nor is he content only with today's successes. He's constantly trying to do what he's never done before. He's learning and growing every day. He knows he may never fully realize his potential, but that doesn't stop him from doing all he can to reach it.

You may love to learn and grow. If you do, I commend you and encourage you to keep doing what you're doing. But if you look at yourself honestly and find yourself in the comfort or coasting zone, I want you to know you can change and become someone who is growing and developing his or her potential. At first it may be difficult, but with each step, the process gets easier and more enjoyable.

Consider areas where you would like to grow, and begin reading books and listening to tapes on those subjects. Go to conferences. Spend time with successful people in those areas. If you don't already have a strategy for development, you may even want to put yourself on the plan for growth in breakthrough #6. You can become the person God intended you to be, no matter how old you are or what your personal history is.

My parents excelled in this area. My father and mother were constantly improving themselves, and they still are. Dad is over 70 at the time I write this, and not long ago, I saw him reading *The Power of Positive Thinking,* by Norman Vincent Peale. "Dad," I said, "what are you doing? You're one of the most positive people I know, and yet you're reading about positive thinking. How many times have you read that book?"

"Oh, I've read this more than a dozen times over the years," he said. "But it's important for me to keep reading it, John. I've got to keep improving myself. I don't want to let myself fall into negative thinking!"

When we were kids, my brother, sister, and I were required to read every day. Our parents expected positive development to be part of our daily experience. And when our parents saw an opportunity for our growth, they seized it. For example, I had a breakthrough when I was about 10 years old that my father later built on. When I was in fifth grade, we studied the judicial system, and our teacher, Mr. Horton, decided we would create a mock court to learn about the process. I chose to run for judge against Bill Phillips, a popular boy whose father drove the school bus.

When I got elected, I was surprised. Mr. Horton congratulated me, and I told him I hadn't expected to win. He put his hand on my shoulder and said, "You're very popular, John. Don't you know that all the kids like you?"

That's when I first realized I had relationship skills, and it motivated me to want to improve them. Dad recognized that, and when I was in seventh grade, he sent me to my first Dale Carnegie course—"How to Win Friends and Influence People"—and he attended it along with me. By the time I graduated from high school, I had completed two Carnegie courses. Dad knew that God was calling me to work with people, so he provided me with growth experiences and helped me develop skills that would bring me closer to reaching my potential.

You can create an environment for growth in your home. Begin by praising your children any time they show a desire to learn. Provide opportunities for them to have new experiences. Buy books and tapes for them. Show them you value growth. Require it from them and yourself. And reward them when they do something that develops their potential. Make it a part of your lifestyle.

Expect Great Things to Happen

A primary limitation in life is our low expectations for ourselves and others. When we expect minimum results, that's usually what we get. Even Jesus told His disciples, "You have not because you ask not."

Because my parents maintained a positive attitude and depended on God for results, they always had high expectations, not only for us, but in everything they did. I remember an incident, for instance, that occurred when I was in college and I sang in the school's quartet. My dad used to drive us four guys to churches to perform. When we finished singing, one of the four of us would preach a salvation message, and then my dad, who at that time had 25 years of experience as a preacher, would give an altar call.

On one of those trips, we went to a little country church that didn't seem to have much life left in it. As we looked over the sanctuary to see where we would perform, Dad noticed a bunch of flowers lined up in the altar area, and he realized they would prevent anyone from coming forward when he gave the altar call. He wanted to move the flowers, but when he asked the pastor if he could do it, the pastor seemed reluctant. "Nobody has received Christ in this church for years. No one will come forward," he said.

But Dad had high expectations for that night. After the pastor left, Dad said, "Come on, boys. Let's move these flowers. You boys are going to give a wonderful performance; Johnny will preach a good message; and God's going to do something wonderful here tonight."

Dad's expectations were high for me and the people of that congregation, as they always were, and his faith was rewarded. Many people came forward that night and received Jesus as their personal Savior.

Help Your Child Develop a Healthy Self-Image

Dr. Joyce Brothers, well-known psychologist and author, said, "An individual's self-concept is the core of his personality. It affects every aspect of human behavior: the ability to learn, the capacity to grow and change, and the choice of friends, mates, and careers. It's no exaggeration to say that a strong positive self-image is the best possible preparation for success in life."

That's true. Why? Because no person can perform in a manner inconsistent with the way she sees herself. When you believe you're a failure, you will fail. If you believe you have little to offer the world, you'll sit back and contribute nothing. On the other hand, when you feel worthwhile and believe you have lots of potential, you'll begin to achieve. It's not *what you are* that holds you back; it's *what you think you're not.* When your image of yourself changes, your performance changes. The better your self-image becomes, the greater the development of your potential.

Our children's image of themselves comes first from us. We have the power to lift them up or tear them down. Counselor Cecil Osborn said, "The young child has no clear picture of himself. He sees himself only in the mirror of his parents' evaluation of himself. . . . A child who is told repeatedly that he is a bad boy, or is lazy, or no good, or stupid or shy or clumsy, will tend to act out this picture which the parent or some other authority figure has given him."

I was fortunate. My parents built such a positive self-image in me that I thought everyone loved me the same way they did. When I left home at age 22 and entered my first pastorate, I was in for a big surprise. But by then, my self-image was so firmly established that it was too late for anyone to destroy it.

> ## It's not *what you are* that holds you back; it's *what you think you're not.*

Margaret and I have tried to pass along a positive self-image to our children. And it has been one of our notable successes in parenting—almost to a fault. Let me illustrate.

When Joel Porter was about 13, he and I went through James Dobson's "Preparing for Adolescence" tape series. We had made a deal that as we listened, either of us could stop the tape at any time to talk. And as we began to listen to the tape on self-esteem, Joel stopped the tape and said, "Dad, I don't want to hurt your feelings. We can listen to this tape, but I want you to know—I have this part down."

You can build your children's self-image, no matter where it stands now. If you're in the habit of making negative or critical comments about your children, start praying for God to change you, and start holding your tongue. Try to find something positive to say about your children every day. Every person has good qualities—after all, everyone is created in God's image. Look for those qualities.

If you continually encourage your children, you'll soon begin to see positive changes in them. Your kids can be like a child I read about. His math teacher was curious about the positive change in the child's performance from one year to the next. When the teacher asked him why it had occurred, the boy said, "It's because I like myself now when I'm with you."

Help your children to like themselves when they're with you.

Look Beyond Your Own Life . . . Invest in the Future

The whole process of seeing our children as they could be, of spotting and encouraging their potential, is really a matter of looking beyond our own lives and investing in the future. Among Abraham Lincoln's writings, the following words were found:

> A child is a person who is going to carry on what you have started. He is going to sit where you are sitting, and when you are gone, attend to those things which you think are important. You may adopt all the policies you please, but how they are carried out depends on him. He will assume control of your cities, states, and nations. He is going to move in and take over your churches, schools, and corporations. . . . The fate of humanity is in his hands.

And the fate of the children rests in our hands.

My parents understood this principle well, and it was nowhere more evident than in their treatment of my brother, Larry, as he was growing up. From the time he was a child, Larry was always interested in making money. He'd sell magazines door to door, and he put me to work doing the same thing. As soon as he could, he got a paper route.

Many parents would have been concerned that their son was becoming too materialistic—especially if one of those parents was a pastor. But my parents

looked beyond themselves and what the neighbors might think of their raising a money-minded son. They saw Larry not as he was, but as he could be.
They encouraged him to cultivate his gifts and talents and to dedicate them
to the Lord. To give you an idea of how good Larry was, let me tell you this:
He earned and saved enough money to buy a new car for cash while he was
still in high school.

When Larry started going to college, he already had the mind of a good
businessman, and he quickly recognized a genuine opportunity. He saw there
was a lot of money to be made in renting apartments to students near the
campus. Immediately, he formulated a sound business plan for buying apartments and renting them at a profit, and then he took that plan to my father.

At that time, my parents' entire financial security was tied up in their
house. But once again, my parents looked beyond their own lives, and they
decided to invest in Larry. They took out a second mortgage on their house
and loaned Larry enough money to buy his first apartment building.

By the time Larry graduated from college at age 21 with his business
degree, he owned several apartment buildings and was already well on his
way to becoming financially independent. And today, Larry uses his resources
for the kingdom of God. He's a trustee at Indiana Wesleyan University; the
director of the RTN radio network, a system of seven nonprofit Christian
radio stations; a past director of Health Care Ministries; and the current
director of World Gospel Missions, organizations that provide direct support
to medical mission programs in developing countries. He's also a board
member of INJOY, my company that teaches and equips Christian leaders
around the world. Larry's influence touches the lives of thousands of people
for Jesus each year.

Larry's success came because my parents saw him not as he was, but as he
could be. And they invested in him so that he could become that person.
They believed in his potential, and they did everything they could to help
him reach it.

Now, I'm not necessarily suggesting you take a second mortgage on the
house for your children. You may not even own a house. But no matter what
your situation, you can help your children reach their potential, becoming
better than they are today.

DEDICATE YOUR CHILDREN TO GOD

Finally, whether your kids are fresh from the womb or freshmen in college, dedicate them to God. When you do, you give God room to work in their lives. You make yourself a partner with Him. And as D. L. Moody said, "If God is your partner, make your plans big."

It isn't always easy to see our children as they can be because we're so close to who they are at the moment. We can't see the potential forest for all the trees that need our immediate attention. Right now, Margaret and I are coping with a male teenage driver who has had his license for less than a year and has already been to traffic court. So far, it hasn't been our favorite phase of his life. But it's temporary. We're not allowing our view of Joel Porter to be totally colored by these immediate occurrences. We discipline him as necessary, but we continue to love him, encourage him, and focus on his potential.

We encourage you to do the same with your children.

Breakthrough #2

Find Your Child's Bent
Before You Get Bent
Out of Shape

The potential breakthrough for the parent . . .
genuine understanding of the child

The potential breakthrough for the child . . .
a strong sense of identity

Before we were married, Margaret and I talked a lot about having children and our plans for them. I especially remember one conversation. We were sitting in my father's car in front of Margaret's house one evening. As we talked, I told her about all the things I wanted to do with our kids: play ball, go to their games, help them become good leaders, lead them to Christ, have them read the outstanding books my dad had me read—I went on and on.

Then Margaret said, "But what if they aren't interested in sports? What if they don't like the same things you like?"

"That's easy," I answered. "We'll just teach them. If we provide them with the right home environment, they'll turn out just like us."

EARLY ENVIRONMENTALISTS

Back then, Margaret and I were environmentalists—not like Jacques Cousteau or the people trying to save the rain forests, but environmentalists when it came to child rearing. We believed surroundings were more important to the way a child turned out than any other factor. We believed we could be given any children, and if we raised them in our home environment, they would turn out exactly like us. I had strong opinions about how kids should be raised; I had two dozen theories about it.

Then God humbled me by giving me children of my own. Now I have two children and no theories.

THE GREAT DISCOVERY

Our daughter, Elizabeth, wasn't with us for long before we made our first great discovery: She was always going to be different from us. While Margaret and I like spending time with others, Elizabeth enjoys time alone. We're doers who enjoy constant activity. She, on the other hand, enjoys downtime when she can think and regroup. We enjoy making decisions, and we make them quickly. But she likes to reflect and process ideas before reaching decisions, and she often puts them off to the last moment.

To tell you the truth, at first we thought something was wrong with her, and we wanted to fix her. But then we discovered a book that changed our thinking. It's called *Personality Plus,* by Florence Littauer. In it, Florence teaches that there are four basic personality types:

Sanguine: *desires fun; is outgoing, relationship-oriented, witty, easygoing, popular, artistic, emotional, outspoken, and optimistic.*

Melancholy: *desires perfection; is introverted, task-oriented, artistic, emotional, goal-oriented, organized, and pessimistic.*

Phlegmatic: *desires peace; is introverted, unemotional, strong-willed, relationship-oriented, pessimistic, and purpose-driven.*

Choleric: *desires power or control; is strong-willed, decisive, goal-oriented, organized, unemotional, outgoing, outspoken, and optimistic.*[1]

People generally fall into one of these personality types, or they have a blend of two types. We discovered that Margaret and I are both blends of choleric. I'm choleric-sanguine, and she's choleric-melancholy. Elizabeth, on the other hand, is phlegmatic-melancholy. Her thinking and actions will always be different from ours in many ways. That was a major discovery for us. We realized she wasn't *wrong,* just *different.*

TRAIN THEM UP IN THE WAY THEY SHOULD GO

Our discovery about Elizabeth gave us new insight into a verse we used for guidance when it came to parenting: "Train a child in the way he should go, and when he is old he will not turn from it" (Prov. 22:6). Before we fully appreciated Elizabeth's differences, we tended to look at that verse the way most people do. We thought it meant, "Train a child in the right way." In other words, take your child to church, teach her to love and obey God, have her memorize Scripture, and then set her on the same path you chose. After all, if it was right for you, isn't it the right way for your child as well?

The answer is, "Probably not." Every child has a particular bent, a set of characteristics created by God (see Ps. 139:13). That bent is the result of the child's temperament, spiritual gifts, interests, physical qualities, and talents. Your child's bent is a unique blend. The differences from you may be subtle, or they may be as obvious as the contrast between night and day. Our responsibility as parents is to recognize a child's bent— "the way he should go"—and then help him along by encouraging and training him according to his makeup and potential.

FORGET TREATING YOUR CHILDREN THE SAME

My mother and father are excellent models of parents who raised their children in the way they should go. For one thing, they recognized that each of us was different, so they treated us differently. Larry, for instance, has a melancholy-choleric personality. As I already mentioned, from the time he was a child, he was interested in money and business. He was a serious student who often made straight A's, usually leading his class. And he loved to work. He had a regular job from the time he was in junior high school, and he became a successful businessman.

On the other hand, my personality is sanguine-choleric. I wasn't very serious in school. I didn't want my parents to get bored with my grades, so I avoided the monotony of straight A's and made sure my report card had a wide variety of letters on it—the most colorful grades always coming in conduct.

As a kid growing up, I enjoyed being around people, and mostly what I wanted to do was play ball and have fun. When I led my class, it was usually into trouble, like the time I was in music class in fifth grade. We had a teacher who used to sit with her back to us and pound away at the piano. That was too much for me to take, especially since I was already a better piano player than she was. One day, I realized I had a real opportunity. As she banged away at the "Battle Hymn of the Republic," I organized the students and marched them stealthily out of the classroom. I peeked through the door and watched as she turned around. She was shocked when she saw no one was there. Boy, did I get into trouble for that one!

And then there's my sister, Trish. She's mostly choleric, with some melancholy thrown in. Her interest growing up was psychology. As an adult, she became a nurse.

It would have been easy for my parents to compare me to Larry in order to motivate me to do better in school. But I never once heard anything like, "Why can't you get good grades like your brother?" When we got our report cards, our parents sat us down individually to discuss our grades. They never expected different children with different gifts and personalities to perform the same as one another.

If you have more than one child at home, resist the temptation to treat them the same. Chances are, they're very different, and that's to be expected. Remember Cain and Abel? One was a tiller of the fields, and the other was a keeper of livestock. Remember Jacob and Esau? Though they were twins, their personalities were remarkably different. The same was true of brothers Absalom and Solomon. One was a rebel, a man of violence. The other was a man of peace, a wise and keen diplomat. In the case of each set of brothers, their parents didn't treat them the same, and neither did God. Love all your children unconditionally, but develop them differently.

> **If you have more than one child at home, resist the temptation to treat them the same.**

DISCOVERY OF YOUR CHILD'S BENT

There are two stages in training your children in the way they should go. The first is discovery. Once you've recognized that your children are different from you (and one another), you must purpose to discover who they really are.

As I began to write this chapter, I thought about the wonderful job my parents did in this area. Larry, Trish, and I became conscious of our gifts and interests early on. While we were still in grammar school, we all knew what we wanted to do with our lives. I asked Mom how she discovered our bents. She said there were three keys:

1. Prayer

On the first Sunday after we were born, Mom and Dad dedicated each of us to God. She claimed the promise of James 1:5: "If any of you lacks wisdom, he should ask God, who gives generously to all without finding fault, and it will be given to him." And on the day we were dedicated, she prayed a prayer like this:

> Lord, we acknowledge You have given us this child. We praise You and thank You, for there is no greater gift You could give us. We now dedicate him to You, placing him back in Your hands.
> We also dedicate ourselves to raising him right—doing the best we can. Lord, You created him, and You know everything about him. Please help us to understand this child. Give us the wisdom we'll need to be good parents who will raise him right. Amen.

Mom and Dad always began every venture with prayer, and they still do. They recognized that without God's help, they could have no success. That was especially true of parenting. *If you've never asked God to give you wisdom in understanding your children, take the time to do it right now.*

2. Observation

Mom's second step in discovering our bents was observation. She was always watching us and learning from it. She watched to see what we liked, what our successes were, where we failed, how we interacted with others, how we behaved when we thought we were alone—you name it.

For instance, she told me that she knew, when I was about six years old, that I was going to be creative based on the way I played marbles. She said I entertained myself for hours. First I'd play war with them. Then I'd shoot marbles, being both players in the game. Next I'd make up a baseball game with them. She saw that I liked to use my imagination all the time, and that was quite a contrast to Larry, who was always more interested in facts and wanted to get to the bottom line.

Margaret and I have also tried to be observant with our kids. The Christmas that Joel Porter was three and a half, for example, he told us he wanted a vacuum cleaner as his present. We thought it was an unusual request, but he loved to help his mom vacuum. He was also unrelenting in his request. So Margaret and I found a vacuum for him at a garage sale for about $10, wrapped it up, and put it under the tree.

On Christmas morning, he was ecstatic. He had little interest in opening his other gifts. He immediately started up the vacuum and began to clean the living room floor. About 30 minutes later, we realized he was awfully quiet, and we went to see what he was up to. We found that he had begun to take the vacuum apart to see how it worked.

That turned out to be an important moment for him and for us. Using his hands, working with tools and equipment, and discovering how things work turned out to be significant to Joel Porter—the kind of activities he gravitated to over and over. That Christmas morning when we saw him taking apart the vacuum, we could have yelled at him for ruining his gift. That would be a parent's natural response. After all, he couldn't have gotten any help from me in putting it back together—my mechanical ability ends with being able to screw in a light bulb.

But we didn't scold Joel. And he was able to put the vacuum back together. That's when we recognized he had a natural curiosity and a gift for anything mechanical. In fact, whenever there's a repair job around the house or something technical that needs to be figured out, we call on Joel.

Proverbs 20:11-12 points out the importance of observation: "The good or bad that children do shows what they are like. Hearing and seeing are gifts from the LORD" (CEV). Watch your children. And as you do, think not about what they're getting into, but about their bent that's coming out.

3. Listening

The final key to discovering your child's bent is listening. My mother was especially strong in this area. In fact, when Dad was the president of Circleville

Bible College and Mom was the librarian, she was like an on-campus mother to dozens of girls at the school. They used to talk to her for hours. And when we were kids growing up, she always had time to listen to us.

Most parents today don't listen to their children as they could. Their busyness and preoccupation with other things prevent them from giving their children the time they need. James Dobson says, "Parental insensitivity is the number one reason for the causes of an unhappy home."

I once read a comment from a boy that represents how many children feel about their interaction with their parents. He said, "You know what I am? I'm a comma. When I talk to my dad, he'll say something, and then when I start to talk, he makes a comma. He doesn't interrupt me, but when I'm finished talking, he starts in right where he left off. It's as if I didn't say anything."

Sometimes you can discover a lot about your child's bent by listening to what he likes to talk about most often. Right now, Joel Porter is 17. Lately, our goal has been to get him to give more than single-word answers to our questions. If you asked him 20 questions ranging from school to girls and anything in between, you might get 30 words out of him. But if you asked him about his favorite subject—lighting for the theater—he'd talk to you for hours. He'd tell you about floodlights, spotlights, klieg lights, gels, wiring, effects—the list goes on and on. Margaret and I have taken him twice to see his favorite play, *Phantom of the Opera*. He doesn't care about the plot, and he couldn't sing you a song from it, but he could tell you how they lit every single scene and what equipment they used to do it.

DISCIPLINE: THE OTHER HALF OF DEVELOPING YOUR CHILD'S BENT

Discovering each child's bent is incredibly important, but it isn't enough—it's only half of the process. Once you've found it, the real question is what you're going to do about it. And that means discipline, the discipline of finding and following through on ways to *develop* that bent. A child's growth depends on three things:

1. Exposure

To help a child develop a bent, you must expose him or her to new experiences based on what you've observed. Even when an activity isn't something the child wants to pursue, in the long run it can still be positive for overall growth. And if it's something that takes, that's even better.

My parents were good models in this area. When my siblings and I were young, all of us took piano lessons because our parents felt it was important that we develop musically. But the process changed for each of us according to our bents. For me, that meant seven and a half years of piano lessons. I really enjoyed music and had some talent to keep me going.

Larry, on the other hand, had little talent and even less interest in music. After three months, they no longer required him to take lessons. And Trish was different from both of us. She had talent, but her greatest instrument was her voice. After a while, Mom and Dad allowed her to stop taking piano and focus on developing her voice.

Margaret and I have tried to expose our children to experiences according to their bents, too. For example, Elizabeth has always been small but athletic. When she was in elementary school, we put her in gymnastics. She really enjoyed it, and she was good at it. When the summer Olympics were scheduled to come to Los Angeles in 1984, I wanted to give her exposure on another level, so I searched for tickets to the gymnastics finals. There were no tickets to be had, but I was determined. It wasn't a matter of *if* I could get tickets for her; it was a matter of *how* I would get them. Everywhere I went, I mentioned I was trying to find them. In the end, some friends who were missionaries, Jim and Diane Gordon, got us tickets through the government of Chile. Margaret took Elizabeth, and she loved it.

There have also been times when exposure to new things wasn't a perfect success. When Joel Porter was a freshman in high school, for instance, he decided he wanted to play football. We had our doubts about how successful he would be. Joel's a good athlete; he enjoys skiing and riding motorbikes. But he tends to excel at sports that don't involve teams, and we weren't too sure he'd take to football. But we allowed him to play anyway, figuring the exposure would be a positive experience overall. However, we did give him one condition. If he started, he had to stay with it for the whole season. He was not going to be allowed to quit.

Well, as it turned out, football was not his favorite activity. He would have been happy if the season had miraculously ended several months early, but of course, it didn't. And he stuck it out. It was important that we didn't prevent him from trying something new just because we were pretty sure he wouldn't like it. We had to let him have failures as well as successes in order to develop his bent.

2. Sacrifice

The second element in developing a child's bent is sacrifice. The concept of sacrifice isn't popular today; people seek security, not sacrifice. But the truth is that there's no success without sacrifice. Any time you experience progress, you or someone before you has sacrificed. And if you're making sacrifices and aren't seeing success, someone else following you will.

The same principle holds true when it comes to raising children. If you want to develop your child's bent, you'll have to answer the question, What am I willing to *give up* to see my child *go up?* Developing your child's bent will probably cost you money and time. It may mean giving up some of your hopes and dreams in order to further hers. How far are you willing to go? What are you willing to give up?

> Any time you experience progress, you or someone before you has sacrificed.

When I think about the sacrifices my parents made, I'm truly grateful. I think about the musical instruments they bought us, even though neither of them was musical. I think about the business trips my dad took me on even though it meant extra work for him (more about that in breakthrough #4). I think about how my parents sent me to two expensive Dale Carnegie courses before I graduated from high school. (They knew I would be in a profession where the ability to work with people was vital.) They were willing to do anything they thought would enhance our potential.

Margaret and I have tried to follow in their footsteps with our children. For instance, when Joel Porter was 10 years old, he decided he wanted to participate in the church's ministries. Specifically, he wanted to help with the technical side of productions and events, particularly with light and sound. We wanted to encourage him in this, but it meant we had to make two 50-minute round trips to the church, a big sacrifice for us considering our busy schedules.

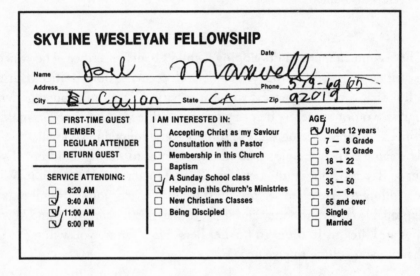

We've made other sacrifices for Joel, too. Because he loves to tinker and work on projects, we've allowed him to have his own workshop. We set aside a part of our garage just for him, and we gave him a budget for finishing it out as a work area. For more than a week, he made phone calls and went to home supply stores, checking on materials and costs. He checked into lumber, wiring, light fixtures, and more. And Paul Nanney, a friend of ours who's a contractor, supervised the construction process. (Paul says Joel has enough wiring in that room for 10 workshops.)

No matter how old your children are, you need to ask yourself what you're willing to give up so they can go up. Each child is different, and the bent of one may require something different from the bent of another. Ask yourself . . .

- What percentage of my budget am I willing to dedicate to developing my child's bent?
- How many hours a week of my free time will I cheerfully sacrifice to develop my child's potential?
- Am I willing to relinquish my own agenda and, for instance, arrange the family vacation around the interests of my child?
- Am I willing to delay buying new clothes, a newer automobile, or a bigger house to increase my child's potential?
- Would I be willing to change jobs or move to another city if that were the only way to develop my child's bent, such as is the case for the parents of some Olympic athletes?

These aren't the only questions you can ask, and there are certainly no right or wrong answers. But recognize this: The greater the sacrifice you're willing to make, the greater the odds of your child reaching his or her potential.

3. Focus on the Child's Interests, Not Yours

Development of a child's bent requires that we become willing to change our focus. It's natural for us to want our children to be interested in the same things that interest us, and when that happens, it can bring boundless joy. But our goal should be to focus on *their* interests, not ours.

In my case, my dad supported my desire to play basketball. He encouraged me to attend Wednesday night basketball practice rather than the midweek service, even though church members criticized him for it. He went to my games whenever he could, and he cheered me on like a basketball fanatic. I remember a day in high school, after one of our games, when a friend came up to me and said, "I sat next to your dad at the game last night."

I was puzzled because I knew I had never introduced my dad to her. "How do you know it was my dad?" I asked.

"Because every time you got the ball," she said, "he shouted, 'Shoot the ball, Johnny! Shoot the ball!'"

She didn't know that my dad knew nothing about basketball and had no innate interest in it. But he was interested in seeing me reach my potential, so he came to the games and cheered me on.

THE MISSING LINK IN PARENTING

Back when I was growing up, my father practiced something that's as crucial to leading a family as it is to leading a business, government office, sports team, or church. It's something he did almost instinctively: He first connected with people on a personal level before he tried to lead them on any other level.

I came to appreciate the importance of establishing this connection later, when I became an adult. As I was teaching leadership to pastors and businesspeople, I realized many of them were trying to lead people with whom they had never connected. They were putting their agenda before the relationship. But that's putting the cart before the horse. To effectively lead people, you must first learn about their interests and dreams. I call this relational connection the missing link in leadership.

The same principle holds true in the home. But unfortunately, I find mothers and fathers doing the same thing with children that bosses do with employees. They try to direct their children without investing in the relationship. But to effectively *direct* your child, you must first *connect* with him. To do that, you have to get on his turf, get his perspective, and find out what's in his heart. When the goal is to control rather than connect with a child, everyone loses.

How connected are you with your child? Have you been putting in the time and energy to build the relationship? Answer the following questions to help you determine the depth or your connectedness:

1. What gives my child joy?
2. Who is my child's hero?
3. What does my child fear most?
4. Which activities give my child energy?
5. Which ones wear my child out?
6. If my child got to choose this year's vacation, where would he or she want to go?
7. If my child could pick one activity for me to do with him or her, what would it be?

8. What music does my child like?
9. Other than going to school or sleeping, what does my child spend the most time doing each week?
10. What does my child want to be when he or she grows up?

If many of your answers are "I don't know" or "Well, when she was five, she wanted to be . . .," you're probably overdue for some connection time. Plan some one-on-one activities with your child. You may want to have a regular date night or Saturday morning activity with each child. One friend used to take each son out to breakfast once a month, with the child choosing the place to eat. He did this from the time his boys were young until they got married and moved out of the house. Any activity is fine as long as your child gets to do some of the choosing (so that you'll be on his turf) and you have some time built into the activity so that you can talk to each other.

WHAT EVERY CHILD NEEDS REGARDLESS OF BENT

Finally, for healthy development regardless of bent, every child needs unconditional love. Only when children feel loved that way can they flourish and grow to meet their potential. Such love provides a nurturing environment. It offers emotional, physical, and psychological security, and it gives children the freedom to fail—and to succeed.

What message are you currently sending to your children? Is it one of unconditional love? Or are your kids likely to believe your love is based on their performance, behavior, compliance, need, or even potential? If it's the latter, you need to start communicating a new message. Your children need to believe your love is based solely on the fact that they belong to you—nothing more and nothing less. And you'll want to communicate that message even when . . .

> they wreck the car.
> they want to drop out of school.
> they need money.
> they wreck the car.
> they blow their most important test.

they cause the team to lose the game.

they wreck the car.

they come home two hours after curfew.

they get into a fight.

they wreck the car!

(Can you tell that Margaret and I have teenagers?)

LEARNING FROM THE PRODIGAL'S FATHER

One of the best illustrations of unconditional love can be found in Luke 15:11-32—the story of the prodigal son. The prodigal's father is our role model as parents. Here's what we can learn from him:

- *He gave his child the freedom to fail.* He divided his wealth and allowed his son to go his own way, even when it meant going the wrong way.
- *He continued to have hope for his child.* He always looked for his son's return, and he saw him from far off.
- *He took the initial steps in reconciliation.* He didn't wait for his son to ask forgiveness before showing his love. Before his son said a word, he ran to him and hugged and kissed him.
- *He expressed unconditional love for his child.* He gave him a place of honor, putting on him the best robe and a ring despite the boy's mistakes.
- *He didn't hold the past over his child's head.* When he saw his son, he never said, "I hope you learned your lesson," "I hope you didn't get anyone pregnant," or "What happened to the money?" He just took him back and loved him.

When the prodigal returned home, he thought he would be doing it as a second-class citizen; he was willing to be a servant rather than a son. But the father wouldn't hear of it. While his son thought second-class, his father was thinking second *chance*.

NO GUARANTEES

As parents, we all hope we won't have to deal with the heartbreak of raising a prodigal child. But as you know, there are no guarantees. The best we can do is love them and try to help them be responsible adults. We've done all we can to help Elizabeth and Joel Porter discover and develop their bents, and so far they seem well aware of their strengths and weaknesses.

When Joel was a high-school freshman, one of his assignments was to write a paper about becoming a missionary. When I read his essay, I was impressed by how mature his thinking was for someone 15 years old and how well he knew himself. Here's part of what he wrote:

> The first qualification is that we need to be saved. The second qualification is to be Spirit-filled. An example of this is Acts 1:8.
> . . . The third qualification is to dedicate yourself completely to God. An example of this is Romans 12:1-2. . . . The fourth qualification is to be called into full-time ministry.
>
> I have fulfilled the first three qualifications. For me to become a full-time missionary, I need to hear the call of God on my life. However, if I am not called into full-time ministry, I still want to serve God.
>
> I have the following qualifications to become a foreign missionary:
>
> 1. I love Jesus.
> 2. I want to see people saved.
> 3. I grew up in a pastor's home, so I understand full-time ministry.
> 4. I have traveled to many foreign countries and understand different cultures.
> 5. I have many skills in working with my hands. Missionaries must be handy in the field. I enjoy working, building, and doing electrical work, etc.
> 6. I enjoy working behind the scenes and would not have to be the head missionary.
> 7. It is not a strength of mine to speak. If God wanted me to

preach, He would have to help me like He did Moses, who was not a gifted speaker.

God would have to give me better emotional qualities than what I have now. First God would have to give me a bigger heart for people. Right now, I enjoy doing projects more than developing relationships with people. [Incredible insight.]

I am willing to say yes to God if He calls me into full-time Christian service. However, if He does not, it is my desire to use my spiritual gifts to help build His church.

We don't know exactly what God will require of Joel Porter, but we're grateful that he has expressed a desire to serve Him. And Margaret and I pray we've given him a sufficient head start in developing his bent so that he can do it to the full extent of his potential.

SEEING THE DIFFERENCES BETWEEN YOU AND YOUR CHILD

If you suspect you've been unaware of how your child is different from you—or you've even tried to minimize or eliminate the differences—complete this survey. If you have more than one child, photocopy it so you can complete one for each parent-child relationship. You may need to answer some questions for your child, such as the one on personality type, but for most, simply ask your child for his or her answer. And remember, there are no right or wrong answers to these questions, so don't judge any answers your child gives or use the test as an opportunity to prompt the answers you'd like to hear.

1. **What is your personality type?**(See page 40 for descriptions.)
   You: Sanguine   Choleric   Melancholy   Phlegmatic
   Your Child: Sanguine   Choleric   Melancholy   Phlegmatic

2. **What gives you more energy?**
   You: Being with other people   Being alone

Your Child: Being with other people   Being alone

3. **Where would you prefer to spend a free Saturday?**
   You: Indoors   Outdoors
   Your Child: Indoors   Outdoors

4. **If you suddenly had $100 and you could do anything you wanted with it, what would you do?**
   You:_____
   Your Child:_____

5. **Who are your heroes?**
   You:_____
   Your Child:_____

6. **If you could play any game, what would you choose?**
   You:_____
   Your Child:_____

7. **When playing or participating in sports, which do you prefer?**
   You: Solo activities   Group or team activities
   Your Child: Solo activities   Group or team activities

8. **What are your favorite physical activities?**
   You:_____
   Your Child:_____

9. **What are your favorite mental activities?**
   You:_____
   Your Child:_____

10. **Which activity brings you close to God most quickly and easily?**
    You: Prayer   Worship   Reading Scripture
    Your Child: Prayer   Worship   Reading Scripture

11. **What are your top three spiritual gifts?**
    You:_____
    Your Child:_____

12. **If you knew God would make it possible for you to live your greatest dream, what would you ask Him to let you do?**
    You:_____
    Your Child:_____

Breakthrough #3

Strive to Be
a Priority Parent,
Not a Perfect One

The potential breakthrough for the parent . . .
a sound strategy for parenting

The potential breakthrough for the child . . .
a deep sense of security

We felt fortunate one recent holiday season because we had a wonderful family Christmas. My parents came to visit, and that was especially significant because my dad experienced a heart attack not long ago, and for a while we feared he wouldn't see another Christmas. My sister, Trish, and her family also celebrated with us because they had moved here to San Diego during the summer. The holidays felt like a family reunion.

One evening, Mom, Dad, Margaret, Trish, Steve (Trish's husband), and I went to our den after dinner to enjoy a cup of tea, a log fire, and the beautiful Christmas tree that Margaret puts up each year. As we sat, we talked—about Ohio, growing up, and how we wished Larry were there to share some of the memories.

It seems that whenever we kids get together, especially if Mom or Dad is with us, we talk about growing up because the memories are so good. On that night, I got to thinking about how my parents raised us. We felt secure because we knew their values. And I began thinking that I wanted to explore what they did so I could share it with you in this book.

"Dad," I said, "you and Mom were really good parents. You seemed to have such clear priorities for us. I wish we were more like you."

"It was easier then," said Mom. "Everything was black and white. It was easier to make decisions. I really feel for parents who are bringing up their children now. It's so much tougher than it was in our day."

"How did you know what was important?" I asked. "Did you list your priorities? That's what Margaret and I did when the kids were little."

"No, Son," Dad said, "we didn't list them, but we lived them."

That was true. I don't ever remember seeing any gap between what my parents asked of us and what they lived themselves. They were consistent, day in and day out—models of good family management. And as NBA head coach Pat Riley said, "Sustain a family for a long period of time, and you can sustain success for a long period of time. First things first. If your life is in order, you can do whatever you want."

NO PERFECT PARENTS

Having such excellent models, Margaret and I determined we would do everything right when we became parents. We would make all the proper decisions. We would ensure that our children exhibited all the right behaviors. We were going be perfect parents.

We couldn't have made a worse decision! There are no perfect parents. And by identifying perfection as our goal, we were setting ourselves up to fail. There are only three kinds of perfect parents: those whose children are grown up and gone and who can't remember what really happened; those who haven't had kids yet; and those who were on television in the 1950s and '60s. Do you remember programs like *Father Knows Best, Ozzie and Harriet, The Donna Reed Show,* and *Leave It to Beaver?* Those parents always had all the right answers, and no problem was ever too difficult to solve during their 30-minute time slot.

Our desire to be perfect parents caused us to make a lot of mistakes early on. When I think back now, I see that what we really wanted was perfect children, and we were trying to produce them by using imperfect methods. For instance, we sometimes compared them to other children in order to get them to behave the way we wanted. We were impatient and expected them to respond to us instantly. We tried to make them just like us. And to make matters worse, we had far too many rules for them. They were often confused because they had difficulty knowing if they were obeying our complex requirements. And that discouraged them.

PRIORITY, NOT PERFECTION

Then one day, we understood that our desire for perfection was hurting our children rather than helping them. It was a Saturday morning. Elizabeth had been playing, and between the two of us, Margaret and I had probably corrected her a dozen times. But correction number 13 was just too much for her. She burst into tears and ran to her room, sobbing, "I can't do anything right!"

Margaret looked at me and said, "John, we've got a problem. If we keep this up, Elizabeth's going to lose all her confidence, and she's never going to want to try anything new."

That's when it struck me. We needed to prioritize what was important to us as parents, just as I had learned to prioritize in most every other aspect of my life. It's something I had learned when I was taking business courses a few years before. It was then that I read about Italian economist Vilfredo Pareto. He taught that we should prioritize the factors in our lives and focus 80 percent of our attention on the top 20 percent of our priorities. When we do that, we get the important things done, and the unimportant ones take care of themselves.

When I first read that principle, I realized that if I followed it, it would change my life. I immediately began using it in my ministry, in leadership, in time management, and so on. But it had never occurred to me to apply it to parenting.

THE MAXWELL LIST OF PRIORITIES

Then Margaret and I set aside some time to talk about what was going to be most important to us as we parented Elizabeth and Joel Porter. My parents had identified a list of 10 qualities that were important to them (see breakthrough #4), but we felt we would be more successful with a shorter list. After a lot of discussion, we narrowed our focus down to five priorities. A couple of the items were on my parents' list; others were not. In the end, we decided that we wanted Elizabeth and Joel Porter to . . .

1. Love and obey God.
2. Have a good self-image.
3. Accept responsibility for their choices.
4. Have a positive mental attitude.
5. Have a thankful spirit.

We decided that if we focused on those priorities and used them to make decisions every day, we would be better parents, and they would be better children.

Love and Obedience to God

Our top priority for our children has been that they love and obey God. My parents claimed a passage in Psalms for us kids, and Margaret and I have also claimed it for Elizabeth and Joel Porter. I'm particularly fond of the way it reads in Eugene Peterson's Bible paraphrase called *The Message:*

> Hallelujah!
> Blessed man, blessed woman, who fear God,
> Who cherish and relish his commandments,
> Their children robust on the earth,
> And the homes of the upright—how blessed!
> Their houses brim with wealth
> And a generosity that never runs dry. (Ps. 112:1-3)

As children, Larry, Trish, and I consistently spent time learning about God and developing a relationship with Him. Although my parents constantly talked with us about spiritual things, our primary learning time was during family devotions in the morning. We had that time every day, and Dad usually led it. He traveled a lot when I was young, but he always tried to get home at night, and he always got up early to lead our devotions no matter how late he arrived the night before.

Dad and Mom kept our devotions fairly short, and they tried to make them fun. We had short prayer times, we read and memorized Scripture, and we played games. One of my favorites was Ten Commandments Trivia. Mom or Dad would recite a commandment and ask us to tell which one it was. Or they'd ask us to recite a commandment word for word. We knew them in order and could recite them backward and forward. They really did become written on our hearts, as Deuteronomy 6:6 says.

Those family devotion times really helped Larry later in life, when he was stationed in Korea during the Pueblo crisis. He told Mom that there were many nights when he was tempted to go out on the town with his army buddies, but instead he stayed in the barracks. He remembered the commandments he'd learned as a child, and he felt strong conviction against the things he knew he would do if he went along with his friends.

Knowing God has made all the difference in my life, as it probably has in yours. And I want the same for my children. I'm reminded of a story I read that was told by business executive Hilding Halverson:

> When my son was a small boy playing with his buddies in the backyard, I overheard them talking one day—and the conversation was amusing, one of those "I can whip your dad" routines. I heard one boy say proudly, "My dad knows the mayor of our town!" Then I heard another say, "That's nothing—my dad knows the governor of our state!" Wondering what was coming next, I heard a wonderfully familiar voice (that of my own little son) saying, "That's nothing—my dad knows God!"

I recently thought about the spiritual legacy my dad passed down to us when I was preparing to speak at Promise Keepers in Houston. They had asked me to speak on becoming a man of God's Word, and as I was planning that message, I got word that my dad had suffered a heart attack. I immediately flew to Orlando to see him, and Margaret and the kids followed soon afterward. The doctors feared he wouldn't survive. When things looked the worst, Larry and I anointed Dad with oil and prayed over him, and he made a significant turn for the better.

I was grateful and filled with joy when I realized he was going to recover, but I did have one regret. I had planned to have Dad with me when I spoke at Promise Keepers, and now he wasn't going to be able to go. As I talked to him in the hospital, he said, "John, I wish I could go with you. You know how much I love to hear you preach. You're talking on becoming a man of God's Word, right?"

"Yeah, Pop," I said.

He pointed to his old, black, well-worn Bible. "Hand me my Bible, Son," he said.

As I picked it up off the nightstand, I noticed the covers were beginning to roll back at the corners due to age and use.

"I can't go with you, but I want you to take my Bible and preach out of it," he told me. "And remember, Son, I'll be praying for you."

Later that night, I grabbed Dad's Bible because I wanted to spend some time in prayer. I opened it and saw Dad had written something on the inside front cover. It said, "Please return to Melvin Maxwell," along with his old address in Circleville, Ohio. And under the address, I found this written:

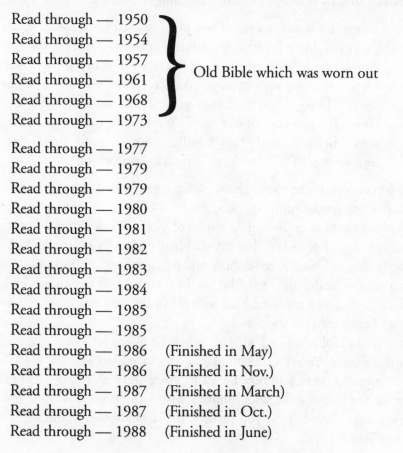

Read through — 1950
Read through — 1954
Read through — 1957
Read through — 1961 } Old Bible which was worn out
Read through — 1968
Read through — 1973

Read through — 1977
Read through — 1979
Read through — 1979
Read through — 1980
Read through — 1981
Read through — 1982
Read through — 1983
Read through — 1984
Read through — 1985
Read through — 1985
Read through — 1986   (Finished in May)
Read through — 1986   (Finished in Nov.)
Read through — 1987   (Finished in March)
Read through — 1987   (Finished in Oct.)
Read through — 1988   (Finished in June)

Read through — 1988	(Finished in Oct.)
Read through — 1989	(Finished in Sept.)
Read through — 1989	(Finished in Nov.)
Read through — 1990	(Finished in June)
Read through — 1990	(Finished in Oct.)
Read through — 1991	(Finished in Feb.)
Read through — 1991	(Finished in June)
Read through — 1991	(Finished in Sept.)
Read through — 1991	(Finished in Dec.)
Read through — 1992	(Finished in May)
Read through — 1992	(Finished in Oct.)
Read through — 1993	(Finished in April)
Read through — 1993	(Finished in Oct.)
Read through — 1994	(Finished in April)
Read through — 1994	(Finished in Oct.)
Read through — 1995	(Finished in Mar.)
Read through — 1995	(Finished in Oct.)

Dad had read through the Bible 38 times! In 1991 alone, he had read through it four times.

The next day I asked Dad, "How did you do it? How were you able to read through the Bible so many times?"

"I refused to read anything in the morning until I first read God's Word," he said.

Two weeks later, I talked to 60,000 men in the Houston Astrodome about becoming a man of God's Word. And I spoke with confidence because I had seen it fleshed out. I knew what a man of God was, because I was raised by a man of God. (I'll cover spiritual growth in more depth in breakthrough #9.)

If you want your kids to love and obey God, give them that same kind of legacy.

A Good Self-Image

In breakthrough #1, I talked about the importance of helping children develop a strong self-image. When children believe they're stupid, lazy, or unlovable, they conform to that image. They become what they think they are. For example, look at what evangelist Bill Glass discovered. He said that 90 percent of all prison inmates were told by their parents, "They're going to put you in jail."

But having a positive self-image has an equally strong effect on children. As Nick Stinnet, dean of Pepperdine University, said, "When you have a strong family, you receive the message that you are loved, cared for and important. The positive intake of love, affection and respect gives you inner resources to deal with life more successfully."

As I mentioned in breakthrough #2, Larry, Trish, and I knew early what direction we wanted to go in life. As a result, we got a fast start on our careers and have been highly successful. Part of that we can attribute to knowing our bents. But we certainly wouldn't have gotten far without the strong, positive self-images developed in us as children. I urge you to do all you can to cultivate such a self-image in your children.

Responsibility for Their Choices

Not long ago, Margaret and I spent a week in New York City on vacation. We shopped, dined, and went to some Broadway shows. We also attended a vespers service at Riverside Church, which was built with money donated by John D. Rockefeller. While we were there, I thought about how Rockefeller tried to give back to the community, and I was reminded of a statement he made that my dad used to quote to us all the time: "Every right implies a responsibility; every opportunity, an obligation; every possession, a duty."

> **While at first we make our choices, as time goes by, our choices make us.**

Responsibility and duty aren't valued and cultivated now as they were when I was growing up. Many people seem to want *others* to be responsible for their choices. They fail to realize that while at first we make our choices, as time goes by, our choices make us. Or as C. S. Lewis said, "Every time you make a choice, you are turning the central part of you, the part that chooses, into something a little different than what it was before. And taking your life as a whole, with all your innumerable choices, you are slowly turning this central thing either into a Heaven creature or into a hellish creature."[1]

Margaret and I have tried to emphasize the importance of choices to Elizabeth and Joel Porter. Like most children, when they were small, their lives were simple, but we always tried to give them choices to get them used to making them. We let them pick their clothes, choose their lunch, decide on leisure-time activities, and so on. We even let them help us choose where to go on vacation sometimes. But in general, their choices were simple.

I'm reminded of one time when I was flying from San Diego to Dallas, and the flight attendant came up and asked if I wanted dinner.

"What are my choices?" I asked.

"Yes or no," she replied.

You can't get any simpler than that!

As Elizabeth and Joel Porter have gotten older, their choices have grown more complex, varied, and significant. And Margaret's and my control over those choices has decreased every day. The ones probably foremost on our minds are their choices about moral purity. A wrong choice in that area can have disastrous consequences.

Because maintaining moral purity and choosing a mate are crucial to the quality of a person's life, we've taught our children about them since they were small. We've talked about what to look for in a spouse (the same priorities listed in this chapter, along with unconditional love for them). We've prayed with them for their future mates. We've discussed the importance of waiting until they're married to have sex.

By the time they became teenagers, they understood that they have the power of choice, but that once they've chosen, their choices have power over them. They knew they must weigh the consequences of their choices carefully.

We've also made some choices that we believe will help them in this area. For instance, they weren't allowed to date until they were 16 years old, and then only in a group. That first year of dating was something of a trial period. If they did well, they would be allowed to go on solo dates at 17. Margaret and I did this because we had seen the statistics and knew that *when* children start dating affects how soon they tend to become sexually active:

Age of Dating	% Having Sex Before Graduation
12	91%
13	56%
14	53%
15	40%
16	20%

Elizabeth and Joel would have liked to begin dating sooner, but even though it wasn't popular with them, we chose to make them wait. When to let *your* kids start dating is a choice you'll have to make, if you haven't already.

A Positive Mental Attitude

One of the subjects I speak about at seminars and special events is attitude. I talk about it because I know that when a person changes his attitude, it literally changes his life. I know because it changed my father's life.

Dad could easily have been a negative person. He grew up in the Great Depression, his mother died when he was six, and he came from a family that didn't have a lot of advantages. He was also born with a melancholy-choleric temperament, which often makes a person pessimistic.

But Dad has always been a very positive person. He's upbeat; he sees the best in people. And growing up, I never once heard him (or Mom) say anything negative about people. I know that's hard to believe, but literally not even once!

As an adult, I came to realize what an accomplishment his positive attitude was, especially since we were trying to instill that quality in our children at the time, and we weren't always successful. One year when we were on a family vacation in Hawaii, Joel Porter was being especially critical, and we were again trying to help him have a more positive attitude. At mealtimes, for example, we required him to find something complimentary to say about each person at the table.

Our difficulty with Joel got Margaret and me talking about my dad. Since he and Mom were with us, we asked him how he had become so positive. He thought about it and discussed it with Mom for a whole day. Then at dinner the next day, he said, "I didn't start out positive. I was the same as most kids—maybe a little worse. But when I was a teenager, I decided I wanted to be successful. So I looked at all the successful men in town, and I realized that regardless of profession, they all had one thing in common. They had positive mental attitudes—every one of them. That's when I decided I was going to be positive, no matter what it took and despite life's circumstances."

One of my favorite positive-attitude stories about my dad happened at a PMA (positive mental attitude) rally back in 1976. Dad took me and my new brother-in-law, Steve, to hear Zig Ziglar, Robert Schuller, Paul Harvey, W. Clement Stone, and other speakers at the University of Dayton Arena. We got there a little late, so when the usher seated us, he put us in the back. The stage was so far away that Kareem Abdul-Jabbar could have been standing up there in place of Robert Schuller and we wouldn't have known it. After a few minutes, Dad said, "Come on, boys. There've got to be better seats than this."

Off we went to find better seats. Dad took us up to the very first row, and his positive attitude was rewarded that day. We found three seats in the middle of the first row—three of the best seats in the house.

As I mentioned, W. Clement Stone was one of the speakers that day. And he made a statement that I've always thought described well the importance of a positive attitude. He said, "There is a little difference in people, but that little difference makes a big difference. The little difference is attitude. The big difference is whether it is positive or negative."

Over a decade ago, I wrote a book called *The Winning Attitude*. One of my favorite parts is something I wrote in my room at the Holiday Inn one evening after speaking at a conference in Houston. Let me share it with you:

What Is an Attitude?

It is the "advance man" of our true selves.

Its roots are inward, but its fruit is outward.

It is our best friend or our worst enemy.

It is more honest and more consistent than our words.

It is an outward look based on past experiences.

It is a thing which draws people to us or repels them.

It is never content until it is expressed.
It is the librarian of our past.
It is the speaker of our present.
It is the prophet of our future.

I created that for pastors and lay people whose lives I wanted to touch. But I also thought about the relevance of those statements for my children, then ages six and four. It was something I wanted to pass on to them.

The value of a positive attitude is almost immeasurable. Its impact is incredible. *But even more incredible is that attitude—mine, yours, and children's—is something we choose.* We may not be able to choose our temperament, our native intelligence, or our physical appearance, but we do get to choose our attitude. Help your children help themselves: Adopt a positive attitude, and encourage them to do the same.

> We may not be able to choose our temperament, our native intelligence, or our physical appearance, but we do get to choose our attitude.

A Thankful Spirit

The final priority Margaret and I identified for our children was a thankful spirit. It's something that was stressed in both our childhood homes. Larry, Trish, and I were required to say thank you any time something was done for us, not just to our parents, but also to each other and people outside the family. We were also required to write thank-you notes when we received gifts and notes of appreciation when a person did something nice for us.

Our parents also modeled gratitude. They constantly thanked God for the blessings they received. They considered all they had a gift from Him. We've tried to pass along that same sense of gratitude to Elizabeth and Joel. We've required them to write thank-you notes and letters expressing appreciation. We constantly thank God for our blessings and ask them to do the same, acknowledging that what we have is the result of His kindness, not anything we deserve.

We've also taken deliberate steps to help them learn gratitude. For example, when I was asked to speak at a Wycliffe conference in Peru in 1987, we made a family vacation of it. And I requested that they fly the whole family into the jungle interior one day to visit a village. I wanted the kids to see how the natives and the missionaries lived.

We left the city early in the morning and flew over what appeared to be an ocean of green as far as the eye could see. After about an hour, we arrived at a clearing that the pilot said was the village we were seeking.

Elizabeth and Joel Porter spent the day playing with the children of the missionaries and the local inhabitants. They saw the people prepare their food in the open and cook over a fire pit. They received gifts from the natives, including a bow and arrow made that day by the tribesmen, as well as the skin of a boa constrictor. They learned a lot about how those people lived and how little they had.

On the trip back to the city, I asked the kids (as I always do when we expose them to new experiences), "What did you like best, and what did you learn?" The thing that impressed them the most was that the children were so happy and so fun to play with—and they had almost nothing in the way of possessions.

Over the years, we've done many things with the kids to help them understand how fortunate they are. One Christmas, we went as a family to the rescue mission here in town and served food to about 3,000 people. The same day, I took Elizabeth, Joel Porter, my nephew Seth, and my nieces Rachael and Jennifer to a shelter for single mothers to hand out gifts. While we were there, a little girl named Samantha followed us around, and Elizabeth observed that she didn't seem to have any shoes. We also met a woman named Mary. She had just given birth to her third child, and she was celebrating. She had done drugs during her first two pregnancies, but she had remained drug-free during the third pregnancy.

The six of us went around talking to the women and their children and giving out gifts. And as we were getting ready to leave, the social worker took me aside and said, "You have a very fine son. I've watched how willingly he helps people."

And then all of a sudden, *I* was feeling grateful.

MEASURING OUR PROGRESS

As I look over our list, I realize we've worked hard at following these priorities and teaching them to Elizabeth and Joel Porter. But if we graded ourselves on the results of our progress, we would not receive all A's. I'd say our report card would look something like this:

Our Report Card	
A-	*Love and Obey God*
A	*A Good Self-Image*
B+	*Accepting Responsibility for Choices*
C	*A Positive Mental Attitude*
B	*A Thankful Spirit*

Our score is far from perfect, but I know we've made a positive impact. We've tried our hardest to live our list. Our children are stronger in these five areas than they would have been if we hadn't made teaching and living them a priority. And my hope is that if we evaluate ourselves on the results 10 years from now, the grades will improve.

SPEND A LONG TIME MAKING A SHORT LIST OF YOUR PRIORITIES

I've discussed our priorities. Now it's time for you to decide on yours. If you're married, it's imperative that you discuss the priorities and agree on them with your spouse. If you and your mate have different priorities, the mixed signals will only confuse your children. Neither of you will succeed in helping them live the priorities, and if your children are smart, they may even play one of you against the other.

If you're not married, you may want to discuss the issues with a wise family member or a friend whose parenting skills you've observed to be excellent. Ask for advice, but don't allow others to make final choices for you.

When you've given it some thought, set aside time that won't be interrupted, and write down possible priorities. You want your list to include only the things that really matter—what you're willing to live and die for. And then you'll want to put them in order of importance.

When you're finished, you should have a list of maybe three to seven priorities. Memorize them. And then put them into practice. When your child does something wrong, ask yourself, Does this violate one of my priorities for my child? If the answer is no and her actions won't harm her or someone else, you may want to let it go. But if the answer is yes, use the correction process as an opportunity not only to address the wrong behavior, but also to teach your child the priority.

LIVING THE LIST

As my dad said, you will want to do your best to live the list, to consistently follow your priorities. If you do, there are wonderful benefits not only for you, but for your children as well. Your ultimate goal is for your children to embrace what you've taught and to make the priorities part of their own list as they become adults.

As we watch Joel Porter growing up, we're beginning to see signs that he's living many of the priorities Margaret and I identified and tried to teach him. In some ways, his teenage years have been tough, particularly the past few months. He's had to work through some difficult issues. In fact, at the last Promise Keepers event where I spoke, I told the men about this book on breakthrough parenting and about how I didn't have all the answers. Then I asked all 65,000 of them to pray for Joel's protection and spiritual growth.

I believe God is already beginning to honor those prayers. Recently, Joel met with members of the Goad Family, the popular Christian musical group. He wanted to work as their lighting technician for their summer tour. As I mentioned in breakthrough #2, Joel loves working in stage lighting. It's his passion, and he has a tremendous gift for it.

It sounded like a great opportunity for Joel, but we wanted him to move slowly, because we knew it would be a big responsibility. So we sent him off to visit the Goads for a couple of days. That way they could assess his technical ability and get to know him. And he, in turn, could get acquainted with them.

After Joel's visit, the Goads told me they were very impressed with him. They said that he not only knew a lot for a 17-year-old, but he knew even more about lighting than some of the technicians who have been working in the entertainment industry for years. He was also able to do some effective lighting effects using the computer. They said they'd love to have him work with them.

Margaret and I thought it over for a week. Joel was already scheduled to go on a short-term mission trip to Kenya during the summer, but we recognized that touring with the Goads was a great opportunity for him. We decided to let Joel go on the road with them for a three-week trial period prior to his trip to Africa. Then we'd see how everything went.

The night before Joel left for Dayton, Ohio, to join the Goads, he wrote a letter to them. He told me he planned to give it to them when he landed in Dayton. But he shared it with me before he left, and I want to share it with you. Here's what it said:

> Dear Goad Family,
>
> I am looking forward to the next couple of weeks with all of you. I have been waiting for this the whole week. I really have been anxious to get out of Ohio and roll up my sleeves to help your family and your ministry. I believe in what you all are doing for the Kingdom of God. That is why I am here. From the two days I spent with your family, you all left an impression on me that will not change. Your whole family has a love for God that does not quit.
>
> I thank you for this wonderful opportunity that you have given me and for believing in a 17-year-old kid. When most people see a 17-year-old, they say, "Oh, he doesn't know anything," and don't invest even a little time to see what he really knows. But your family didn't do that. I felt that your family wanted to listen to what I had to say. I thank you again for this opportunity. I will do my best in what you ask me to do.
>
> I think this is also a chance for me to grow spiritually and to have a bigger heart for people who are hurting—like your family

has a heart for hurting people. I feel for people who are needy, but sometimes I think that diminishes because I am afraid of what other people my age will think. I am going to do what is right for God and what He would want me to do.

Your Friend,
Joel Maxwell

I believe Joel will grow spiritually from this experience. His desire to love others and his intention to obey God show that a work is happening in his life. And it also shows that more and more, he is beginning to act on his beliefs.

As a parent, it's one thing to teach a list of priorities, but it's another to see your kids start to live them out. We may not always see the progress we desire in our children, but when we do, it gives us real joy. Our hope is that each of them will live a life based on solid principles. In time we'll know. And in another 10 years, we'll get that updated report card.

Breakthrough #4

Your Child's Most Important Teacher Is Not in the Classroom

The potential breakthrough for the parent . . .
empowerment

The potential breakthrough for the child . . .
mentoring

A significant event happened when I was in the fourth grade. It was right after lunch in Mrs. Tacy's class. We were going over the nine times table—which by then I could do in my sleep—when I looked up and saw my dad walk into the room. I could feel my face turning red and my heart pounding as I tried to think of what I might have done wrong. Mrs. Tacy had asked me to stop talking a couple of dozen times, but I hadn't gotten into any serious trouble. In fact, I had been unusually good—not out of design, but because no clear opportunities for disruption had presented themselves to me.

"Mrs. Tacy," I heard my dad say, "I'm going out of town tomorrow, and I'm going to take John with me for a few days and teach him."

I couldn't believe it. I was going to get to miss school *and* spend time with Dad! I about jumped out of my chair to celebrate.

Dad continued, "You've been doing a real good job teaching him, but you've had him long enough. It's my turn for a while." Then he turned to me and said, "I'll see you at home tonight, John."

In all my life, I don't ever remember the clock moving as slowly as it did that afternoon. When three o'clock finally came, I was already out the door and running home before the bell finished ringing. When Dad got home that night, I learned that the two of us were going to Pennsylvania, and Mom had already packed a bag for me, just as she did for Dad. I didn't fall asleep for a long time that night, thinking about how I was getting ready to go on my first business trip. Little did I know that I would later log more than two and a half million air miles on the road as a speaker.

What I remember most about that trip was the drives in Dad's Ford Fairlane. We talked for hours about anything and everything: baseball, basketball, current events, music, church, school, and my friends. It's the first time I remember having Dad all to myself for days.

We also got to stay in motels, which was a big deal back then, and we saw the country. Pennsylvania looked different from Ohio—it had lots of mountains and hills, and the trees weren't the same, either. And as we traveled to the various churches my dad oversaw as the district superintendent, I met a lot of interesting people. We got to see some of the Amish country, too. Before then, I thought the only people who traveled by horse and buggy were on TV shows like *Gunsmoke*.

THE MEANING OF EDUCATION

That trip with my dad when I was 10 really made me feel important and grown up. It also set the tone for how he took charge of my education. He and my mom recognized that they were my most important teachers. They valued the teaching we received in school, but they didn't want us to be restricted to that. They knew there was a difference between schooling (acquiring knowledge) and life learning (developing wisdom). Oscar Wilde said, "Education is very admirable, but let us not forget that anything worth knowing cannot be taught." I think he was partly right. I'd say the best things worth knowing are often found outside the classroom.

> Instead of pushing facts in, a true education uses experiences to draw a person out.

Education is so misunderstood. The word *education* has a Latin root meaning "to draw out." Instead of pushing facts in, a true education uses experiences to draw a person out. That's what my father's trips did for me. He mentored me, exposed me to new experiences and ideas, and helped me find talents and gifts within myself. What I learned was relevant; I acquired it in a real-life context; and I got to apply what I learned as I went. The experiences he gave me really drew me out.

WATCH OUT FOR EXPERTS

Many parents are intimidated by educators. Parents have been led to believe that people who barely know their children are much better qualified than they are to decide what their children need. Attending a few years of college or acquiring an advanced degree doesn't automatically make a person wise. There are as many fools with degrees as there are wise people. And both the wise and the foolish write and publish books on education.

There are many outstanding teachers, and I don't mean to disparage their work. But I also want you, as a conscientious parent, to be confident in your knowledge of your child and what's usually best for him or her.

I once read a wonderful piece that gives insight into the value of what some experts have to say:

According to the Book

Junior hit the meter man; Junior hit the cook.
Junior's antisocial (according to the book).
Junior smashed the clock and lamp; Junior hacked a tree.
(Destructive trends are treated in chapters 2 and 3.)

Junior threw his milk at Mom; Junior screamed for more.
(Notes on self-assertiveness are found in chapter 4.)
Junior tossed his shoes and socks out into the rain.
(Negation: that is normal; disregard the strain.)

Junior set Dad's shirt on fire; upset Grandpa's plate.
(That's to get attention — see page 38.)
Grandpa seized a slipper and turned Junior cross his knee.
(He's read nothing but the Bible since 1923.)

If you're easily intimidated by the experts, keep in mind something Tony Campolo's wife used to do at functions attended by educators and other professionals. (He was a college professor; she was a homemaker.) When asked what she did for a living, she would answer, "I am socializing two homo sapiens in the dominant values of the Judeo-Christian tradition in order that they might be instruments for the transformation of the social order into the teleologically prescribed utopia inherent in the echelon." Then she would ask, "And what is it that you do?" When the person answered with something like, "I'm a professor" or "I'm a lawyer," it wasn't as intimidating.[1]

THREE APPROACHES TO TEACHING

Because you know your children well, you know some things they need. Many of those they will never get in school. That's why you must recognize you're their primary teacher. If you don't take responsibility for teaching them what you consider important, they may never learn it.

My parents recognized their role and fulfilled that responsibility in three ways:

Daily Discipline

A vital part of a good education is the discipline of daily learning. As I mentioned before, we had family devotions every morning to aid us in our spiritual growth. But that wasn't all. Every evening from 5:00 to 6:30 was set aside as a family time when we ate dinner and talked. No one missed it. No matter how much work Dad had to do, he was home at 5:00—even if it meant returning to the office after dinner to get his work done. And we kids knew we weren't to come home late or to ask if we could eat at a friend's house. We were to be home.

Those dinnertimes created strong emotional bonds between us. But they were also times of learning. Each of us got the opportunity to discuss what had happened during the day, and my parents helped us work through any difficulties. We learned judgment from hearing good judgment. We learned about the world as we discussed current events. We talked about our relationships with our friends.

We also learned what was appropriate and what wasn't. It was at dinner that Larry told his first dirty joke, for example. When he finished, Mom's eyes were wide, but Dad calmly looked at him and said, "Larry, that's not the kind of humor we use. And that is certainly not how to talk in front of a lady," indicating our mother. "Ephesians 4:29 says, 'Let no corrupt communication proceed out of your mouth, but that which is good to the use of edifying, that it may minister grace unto the hearers.'

"That kind of talk isn't edifying. Do you understand, Son?"

Larry's face was bright red, but he managed to say, "Yes, sir," and we all continued with dinner.

I really enjoyed our dinnertimes, and I discovered something else about them from Trish when my parents were visiting at Christmas. When we used to sit down to eat, Trish was always the last person to the table. Back then, I never thought anything about it. After all, she was seven years younger than me and a girl, which meant she wasn't as fast or as hungry as Larry and me. But after all those years, she told us there was a reason she was always late. Every night as we were getting ready to sit down to dinner, Trish would sneak into our parents' bedroom and take the phone off the hook. And after dinner, she'd sneak back and hang the phone up so that no one ever knew about it. Those dinners were so important to her that she didn't want them interrupted by anyone!

Margaret and I have also tried to use dinner as family time with Elizabeth and Joel Porter, but we've had difficulty doing it because of our schedules. So we've tried some other things. We've had morning and bedtime prayers. And before they were driving age, I always drove them to school in the morning so I'd have time with them. Margaret also used to make driving time a teaching time by having their devotions in the car while she was running errands.

Your schedule and lifestyle may determine what you can do with your children, but the important thing is to schedule some time *daily* for discussion and teaching. The teaching process and the relationship you build need that continuous attention. Otherwise, there may come a day when you find your children have pulled so far away from you that it's hard to reconnect.

Strategic Instruction

The second way my parents took charge of my education was by arranging special events to help me learn and grow, such as the trip to Pennsylvania. That was the first of many tours I took with my dad. He knew I wanted to become a pastor, so he took me with him often when he was visiting churches and helping pastors. I learned more about the church and leading a congregation on those trips than I did from the nine years I spent earning three degrees in Bible college and seminary.

Those tours continued through high school and even into college. For instance, when I was a high-school senior, Dad took me on a two-week trip to Mexico. It was partly a reward for graduation, but it was also a special time when we talked about college and my future. It really helped me to make the transition from high school to college life.

Then when I was in college, Dad sometimes traveled with me and the other members of the college quartet. As we drove, the other three guys would ask Dad dozens of questions—about life, school, people, pastoring a church, and so on. And I learned from his answers, too.

My parents also included other kinds of strategic instruction. For example, when I was in junior high and high school, Dad occasionally took me out of school for the day so I could attend seminars and conferences. I got to hear some powerful preachers and communicators, and I even met and talked with men like Norman Vincent Peale and E. Stanley Jones.

We've taken similar steps with Elizabeth and Joel. I can't begin to count the number of speakers and top-notch preachers we've taken them to see. And we've taken them on lots of trips. Early in our marriage, Margaret and I decided that when my responsibilities required me to travel to someplace interesting, she would come with me, even if it was difficult financially. We knew we needed to continue to grow *together*. Later, when we had the children, we decided we would take them on any trip that would help them grow—again, even when it was difficult financially. Over the years, they've visited more than 25 countries on five continents, and those trips have given them an education they couldn't have received in school or from us.

Lifestyle Modeling

Of all the education I received from my parents, the most significant was their modeling. They consistently lived out the things they taught. And modeling is the most lasting way of teaching. As Abraham Lincoln said,

> **If our words say one thing and our actions another, our children will ultimately follow our actions.**

"There is just one way to bring up a child in the way he should go, and that is to travel that way yourself."

If our words say one thing and our actions another, our children will ultimately follow our actions. I once read a poem that I think captures the spirit of how our children are shaped by who we are:

Children Live What They Learn

If a child lives with criticism,
He learns to condemn.
If a child lives with hostility,
He learns violence.
If a child lives with ridicule,
He learns to be shy.
If a child lives with shame,
He learns to feel guilty.
If a child lives with encouragement,
He learns confidence.
If a child lives with praise,
He learns to appreciate.
If a child lives with fairness,
He learns justice.
If a child lives with security,
He learns faith.
If a child lives with approval,
He learns to like himself.
If a child lives with acceptance and friendship,
He learns to love the world.[2]

That reminds me of something that happened with Joel Porter when he was small. We've stressed with both kids how important it will be for them to love their spouses once they get married. But we know that just telling them isn't enough; they also have to see it. Margaret and I have always been affectionate with one another, and we've never hidden that from the children. One day when Joel Porter was about six years old, Margaret and I were in the kitchen, kissing. He came bursting in, and when he saw us he said, "Are you guys falling in love again?" Even at that age, he understood how we felt about each other.

PRINCIPLES MY PARENTS TAUGHT ME

I learned a lot from my parents: I know I wouldn't be where I am today if it weren't for their love, encouragement, and teaching. Not long ago, I asked them to list the top 10 principles they wanted to teach us as we were growing up. Here's what they identified:

1. Responsibility

As early as I can remember, we were taught to be responsible. As soon as we could walk, for instance, Mom required that we pick up our own toys and put them away. She says it would sometimes take close to 30 minutes as she led me by the hand and I picked up blocks, stuffed animals, and other toys and put them into the huge toy box in the bedroom. It would have taken her about three minutes to do the job, but she invested the time to help me do it, often over the protests of Larry, who wanted to pick them up for me. And her investment paid dividends. I learned to pick up after myself for the rest of my life.

Unlike Larry and Trish, I wasn't a naturally responsible kid. I always preferred to play rather than work. But I was helped by the system my dad used for having us do chores. Every Sunday, he let us know what our responsibilities were for the week ahead. Some tasks were ongoing responsibilities that were to be performed every day by the same person. Washing the dishes, for example, was Larry's and my job, and we did it every night immediately after dinner. Other jobs were assigned occasionally, and we had the freedom to do them whenever we wanted as long as they were completed by noon on Saturday. As our reward, we got to participate in a fun family activity. But anyone who didn't do the assigned chores had to stay home to finish them. That system helped us learn to make good choices and manage our time well.

I remember one particular week that my dad had assigned me the job of cleaning out the basement, a task I hated. Two of my favorite things in life were being outside and being around people, so working in a dark basement by myself was not my idea of fun. That's why I put off doing the job. After a couple of days, I forgot about it altogether—until Saturday noon rolled around.

Mom had made a special picnic lunch, with fried chicken and potato salad, and Dad was getting the car packed for all of us to go swimming. I decided I just wouldn't mention the basement. Then later, when we got home, I'd quietly sneak downstairs, do a little straightening, and no one would be the wiser.

I had my towel in my hand and was headed for the car when I heard Dad say, "Johnny, before we leave, I think you and I need to go down and take a look at that basement."

I was devastated. Dad led the way, and I walked slowly behind him, dragging my towel on the dusty, wooden steps.

"Some tools over there haven't been put away," he said as he began his inspection. "And I see trash over in that corner that ought to have been put out. And those old sheets were supposed to be torn into rags and put into the rag bin."

Then he kneeled down so he could look me in the eye. "You didn't clean this basement, did you?" he asked.

There was no denying it, so I admitted I hadn't.

"When were you supposed to have this basement clean?" he asked.

"Today at noon."

"And what's the rule if you don't?"

I started to cry. "If you don't have your chores done, you have to stay home and do them," I answered.

"Son, I'm really sorry you have to stay home this afternoon," he said. "I love you, and I really wanted you to come swimming with us. But it's very important that you learn to follow through on your responsibilities. This time, you chose to put them off. I hope next time you choose to do your chores on time so you can play with us on Saturday." Then he asked if I understood, and when I said yes, he gave me a big hug.

I still remember the sight of my family pulling out of the driveway, with Trish sticking her tongue out at me. I spent the rest of that afternoon cleaning the basement while everyone else swam and had fun. I learned my lesson, and I got my chores done on time after that. I couldn't stand missing out on our Saturday outings. My parents' system helped even someone as carefree as I was to be responsible. It motivated me and held me accountable.

2. Stewardship

Mom and Dad taught us early the promise in Malachi 3:10—that we were to "bring the whole tithe into the storehouse" and that God would "throw open the floodgates of heaven and pour out so much blessing that you will not have room enough for it." They told us that everything we had belonged to God and that our job was to take care of what He gave us—to be good stewards. Part of that meant giving back to God at least 10 percent of what He gave us.

I can't remember a time when we didn't tithe. When we were kids, we got 50 cents allowance each week, which was more than most of our friends received. We were expected to give five cents of that back to God on Sunday. And my parents tried to make that as easy as possible for us, including giving us our allowance in nickels so we had the right change. It was up to us whether we wanted to give more.

Dad likes to tell the story about what happened one Sunday. During the offering at church, as the plate went by, Mom put her tithe in, and Trish and I dropped in our nickels. But Larry gave 30 cents.

After the service, Dad asked Larry why he had put in the additional 25 cents.

"I got all A's on my report card this quarter," Larry said. "I wanted to give Jesus an extra quarter to thank Him for helping me."

Winston Churchill once said, "We make a living by what we get, but we make a life by what we give." My parents modeled that for us in their living and giving. I know there are differences of opinion among Christians about tithing, but there's no doubt that God wants us to give faithfully and cheerfully (see 2 Cor. 9:6-8).

3. Determination

My dad loves thought-provoking sayings, and he quotes them constantly. One of his favorites is by Abraham Lincoln: "Always bear in mind that your own resolution to succeed is more important than any one thing." Dad not only quotes that saying, but he has also lived it. He has experienced great success in life despite humble beginnings. He has faithfully served God for more than 50 years, including as a denominational superintendent and college president, jobs not ordinarily offered to a man without an advanced degree. He married well and raised three children on a limited income. And his determination has helped him maintain a positive attitude despite some negative circumstances.

My brother, sister, and I shared that same kind of determination when we were kids. For example, when Trish was in junior high school, she wanted very much to play the saxophone. But Mom and Dad were reluctant to buy her one because when they priced the instrument, they discovered a sax cost more than $300 (and they were making only $12,000 a year). But Trish was persistent. She talked to them again and again, promising that if they got her a saxophone, they wouldn't regret it. She said she would study hard and learn to play it well enough to be in her high-school and college bands. Finally, they made the investment, and the thing that convinced them was her determination.

That same sense of resolve has served all of us well in adulthood. Among other things, it helped Trish get through nursing school; it contributed to Larry's success in business; and it has kept me going in the face of overwhelming responsibilities.

4. Potential

I already said so much about potential in breakthrough #1 that I don't need to add much here. But I do need to tell you that my parents practiced Colossians 3:21, which says, "Parents, don't come down too hard on your children or you'll crush their spirits" (*The Message*). They constantly built us up, encouraging us and instilling in us a desire to reach our potential. That desire continues to be a driving force in our lives even today.

5. Relationships

I attended Circleville Bible College, of which my father was the president. I remember one day when I met him at the library, and we walked across campus together to his office. We weren't 10 feet outside the library door when Dad stopped to say hello to a student. He gave him a warm handshake and pat on the back, asked how his parents were doing, discussed his studies, and encouraged him to persevere. As he finished talking to that student and we began walking again, he saw another student and talked with her. This kept happening until we were in his office. What should have been a five-minute walk at most had taken more than 30 minutes.

That's the way my parents were. They put relationships high on their list of priorities. They modeled a good relationship with one another and the people around them. And they encouraged us to work on our relationships at home. Whenever we disagreed on anything, they sat us down and had us talk things out.

Mom and Dad continually stressed the importance of relationships, emphasizing the two that they said would have the greatest impact on our lives: our relationship with Christ and our relationship with a spouse. I accepted Jesus as my Savior when I was three, and my parents continued to help me develop that relationship until I got married and left home.

From the time I was in grammar school, they also talked about the importance of who I would marry. There were times when Larry and I dated girls who weren't good for us, but as I later found out, Mom had a strategy for that. She spent more time on her knees and prayed them out of our lives. It obviously worked, because today all three of us kids have great mates and healthy marriages.

6. Work Ethic

My dad grew up during the Great Depression. At a time when huge numbers of people couldn't find work, he sometimes held down two or three jobs at once. He would go to a business where he wanted to get a job, and he would meet with the owner and make him an offer.

"I'd like to work for you today for free," he'd say. "Put me to work on anything you need done, even the worst job in the place. At the end of the day, if you want to hire me, great. If you've got no place for me, then I'll be on my way, and you'll have gotten a good day's work for nothing."

Dad said he worked a lot of free days, but he also got jobs when he needed them. He has always said there's work to be had by anyone who wants it bad enough. His mind-set reminds me of something I recently read by Sam Levenson: "I learned from experience that if there was something lacking, it might turn up if I went after it, saved up for it, worked for it, but never if I just waited for it. Of course, you had to be lucky, too, although I discovered that the more I hustled, the luckier I seemed to get."

> We can play now and pay later. Or we can pay now and play later. And when we wait until later to pay, the price is usually higher.

Dad and Mom's example was good for us, but they also taught us to work. When we came home from school, we were required to do our homework before we played. And we always had chores to do, as I mentioned before. As we got older, we worked more and played less.

As I said in breakthrough #1, my parents taught us the concept of "pay now, play later." We can approach our responsibilities in one of two ways: We can play now and pay later, or we can pay now and play later. The choice is ours, but no matter what we do, at some point we'll be required to pay. And when we wait until later to pay, the price is usually higher.

Once I learned that lesson, it became a pattern in my life, and it has helped me to achieve a lot. Margaret and I delayed our wedding until I finished college, which gave me a head start in my pastoral career. I was offered a choice of two positions when I graduated, and I accepted the smaller rural church, which benefited me later because I learned the job from the ground up and developed as a leader.

I read an editorial in *U.S. News & World Report* that shows how crucial it is to instill this concept in our children:

> They call it the marshmallow test. A researcher gives this choice to a 4-year-old: "I am leaving for a few minutes to run an errand, and you can have this marshmallow while I am gone, but if you wait until I return, you can have two marshmallows."
>
> Researchers at Stanford University ran that test in the 1960s. A dozen years later, they restudied the same children and found that those who had grabbed the single marshmallow tended to be more troubled as adolescents. Astonishingly, the one-marshmallow kids also scored an average of 210 points less on SAT tests.[3]

The ability to delay gratification and develop a strong work ethic is a tremendous advantage in life.

7. Attitude

You already know how important I think a positive attitude is. I learned that from my dad. For instance, when I was in junior high, Dad pulled me out of school one day so I could hear Harry Blackburn speak. He was a fantastic motivator. At the end of his speaking time, he spat in the palms of his hands, clenched his fists, and began to shadowbox. As he moved around, he recited this poem:

> If you think you are beaten, you are.
> If you think you dare not, you don't.
> If you'd like to win but think you can't,
> It's almost certain you won't.
> Life's battles don't always go
> To the stronger or faster man,
> But sooner or later, the man who wins
> Is the man who thinks he can.

When he finished, the entire audience was on its feet, clapping and cheering, including me. I turned to Dad and said, "That's us, Dad, isn't it?"

"Yes, John, it is," he said with a smile.

8. Honesty

Thomas Jefferson called honesty the first chapter in the book of wisdom, and I'm sure my parents would agree. I count both of them wise; there was always consistency between their words and actions, and I could depend on them to be honest with me about anything.

When I was a freshman in college, starting to prepare for ministry, God spoke to me during a prayer time. I felt convicted about some acts I had committed as an adolescent, ones He reminded me were dishonest. I asked God for forgiveness, but I sensed that there was something else for me to do, though I wasn't sure what. So I went to my parents, explained the whole thing to them, and asked their advice.

"Son," my dad said, "if you want to set things right, you need to make restitution. You need to go to each person you've offended, ask forgiveness, and pay whatever you owe."

"That's right, Honey," added my mom. "If you're going to be an effective spiritual leader, you need to have a clean slate, not only with God, but also with the people you've injured."

"I did the same thing myself when I was a young man," said Dad. "It was very difficult, but it has also helped me. There have been times in my life when I've been tempted, but then I thought about having to make restitution again and how hard it was. That's helped me stay honest."

The next day, I decided to follow their advice. First I went to Boyer Hardware, where I'd had a part-time job in high school. Back then, I had taken home some things without thinking, and I had never bothered to bring them back: pens, a tape measure, a work apron. I returned the items that day and apologized for having taken them.

Next I went to Gallagher Drugstore to apologize and pay them the cost of a magazine. One day in high school, I had seen a sports magazine there that had a great basketball article in it, and I just took it. I also went to Paul's Grocery and paid for an RC Cola I had stolen.

My final stop was back at my high school. Over the course of four basketball seasons, I had taken home uniforms, sweats, and other things like that. So I collected all those items and took them back to Coach Neff. When I walked into his office adjacent to the locker room, he was surprised to see me. He was even more surprised when I explained that I was doing this because I felt God wanted me to.

Making restitution had an incredibly freeing effect on me and made me want to continue living a life of integrity. But it had an impact on more than just me: About 10 years later, when I was a pastor in Lancaster, Ohio, I was working in my office one day when someone came to visit me. It was my old coach, Don Neff. He had some questions he wanted to ask about God. I believe he came to me for answers because he remembered that day 10 years earlier. Before he left my office, he accepted Jesus as his Savior. The modeling of my parents in the area of honesty helped to usher him into the kingdom of God.

9. Generosity

I grew up in a pastor's household, which meant we weren't rich. But I never knew that. Let me tell you a story to illustrate.

One day in fourth grade, we were learning graphs, and Mrs. Tacy was teaching us using an illustration that charted the annual incomes of the students' families. She asked all of us to raise our hands and said, "I'm going to start here on the graph at $5,000. When I get to the number that corresponds to the amount of money you think your family earns, I want you to put down your hand."

It wasn't long before most of the kids' hands were down. After all, we lived in a rural community. But as she kept going, my hand stayed up, even when the children of lawyers and doctors put theirs down. Because of my parents' generosity, I thought we were the richest people in town. They were always giving and expecting nothing in return. And at home, we certainly had everything we needed.

Generosity is something that's been ingrained in all three of us kids. Recently, I came across something I wrote in 1979. It was my definition of success: "Success is choosing to enter the arena of action determined to *give yourself to that cause which will better mankind* and the lost for eternity." Then I looked through my files for a more recent success statement that I had written (1992):

> Success is . . .
>> KNOWING God and His desires for me;
>> GROWING to my maximum potential;
>> SOWING seeds that *benefit others.*

What struck me was that both statements, though created 13 years apart, included giving as a basic part of success. I credit that attitude to the teaching of my parents.

10. Dependence on God

The final—and most important—principle taught to me by my parents is dependence on God. "Cast thy burden upon the LORD," Mom used to say, "and he shall sustain thee; he shall never suffer the righteous to be moved" (Ps. 55:22, KJV).

One of Dad's favorite phrases while I was growing up was "Without us, God will not; without God, we cannot." And he used to love to quote John 15:5: "Without me [Jesus] ye can do nothing" (KJV).

I remember the first time Dad and I were going to preach together. It was one of the first times I sang with the college quartet. The evening was planned like this: The quartet would sing, one of us would deliver a short message, and Dad would give the altar call. For that particular service, I was to give the sermon, and I was feeling nervous because I truly wanted to see people come to Christ.

The five of us gathered in the auditorium to pray before the service, and Dad prayed something that I'd heard him say many times before, but it especially connected with me that night. He said, "God, if You don't come, nothing of value will happen." His statement made me realize that I should do my best, but my actions were not going to make the difference. Only God could do that. It's something I've tried to remember—and acknowledge in prayer—ever since.

THE STAGES OF A CHILD'S DEVELOPMENT

As you think about taking charge of your children's education, know that at different ages, your children need different things from you. I've found that there are three general stages of development in a child's life, and different strategies need to be used for each.

The Age of Regulation (0-7)

When children are small, they act based on their feelings more than on logical thinking. That's why their strongest need is for *instruction*. We ought to provide rules and consistent expectations. In return, we should require obedience. And when children are disobedient—as they will be—we should try to look at those times as opportunities to explain what they did wrong and why.

When Joel Porter was a preschooler, we realized he had a strong bent for lying. So whenever we caught him in a lie, we used it as a teaching time, explaining that God demands honesty. And we reinforced that teaching with Scripture. The first verse we ever taught Joel was Proverbs 12:22: "Lying lips are an abomination to the LORD" (NASB). When Joel recited it, he had trouble with *abomination*. He used to say "a-bomb-damnation," but we accepted his pronunciation because we could tell from his demeanor that he knew lying was a very bad thing.

The Age of Imitation (8-12)

As children get older, they listen less to what we say and are inclined more and more to imitate what we actually do. At that point, their greatest need is *demonstration* of what we want them to learn. That's one reason my father didn't start taking me on trips until I was in fourth grade. Before then, they wouldn't have made such an impact on me. But his timing was perfect, and he influenced me profoundly. I saw him model good relationships, a strong work ethic, a positive attitude, generosity, and many more things on the road. I wanted very much to be like my dad, and in many ways, I still do.

The period from 8 to 12 years old is also the prime time to encourage children to read. If we were to survey any group of highly successful people, we would find that the majority of them read constantly. We would also find that most of them learned to love reading between the ages of 8 and 12. If your children are in this age range (or soon will be), help them enjoy reading and become better readers. (I'll talk more about this in breakthrough #6.)

The Age of Inspiration (13 and up)

The third stage in our children's development is a period of questioning and doubt. Our children know what we believe and what we're likely to do in nearly any situation. But when they reach adolescence, they begin asking themselves, *What do I want to do? Should I do what my parents do, or should I try something different?*

That's why *exposure* is so important at this time in their lives. They're looking at their options. The people they meet and the things they see show them some of the possibilities. It was during this time that Dad most often took me to hear speakers and meet devoted men and women of God. He wanted me to see the kind of person I could become.

During this period in children's lives, goals are very helpful. Long- and short-term goals provide stability and promote character. Auditioning for a band, making the cut to play on a sports team, or saving to buy a hobby item can each be a good goal. Vocational goals can also be excellent. Joel Porter, for example, recently came to Margaret and me with a plan for a professional lighting business he wanted to start in the next year or two. It included buildings, a big-rig truck, and millions of dollars of lighting equipment. We praised him for having goals, but we also had to explain that his plan was a tad overambitious. We hope he'll start his business someday, perhaps on a more modest scale, but in the meantime, we're glad he has worthwhile goals.

The bottom line is that you want to help your children develop character and values as they mature. The values you pick are up to you (and your spouse if you're married). Begin by looking at the ones my parents used and the priorities I talked about in breakthrough #3. Some of those will undoubtedly correspond to the values you embrace. Choose what's important to you, add anything that may be missing, and you've got your list. Just remember—your goal is to prepare them for the time when they will be making all their own choices. That's the real value of education. And it's not something you can do alone. You'll need help. That's the subject of breakthrough #5.

Breakthrough #5

Don't Parent Alone

The potential breakthrough for the parent . . .
added support

The potential breakthrough for the child . . .
added value

When I was 13 years old, I had one of the greatest teachers in the world. His name was Glenn Leatherwood, and he taught seventh-grade-boys' Sunday school. When I think back on it now, I realize our class was a squirrelly bunch—as only seventh-grade boys can be. We were constantly wiggling and giggling and cutting up. But Mr. Leatherwood had a way with us. Sometimes in class, he would stop teaching the lesson and tell us how much he loved us and cared about our relationship with God. Even ornery kids like us stopped poking and punching one another long enough to listen.

One Sunday in particular from that year stands out in my memory. Mr. Leatherwood was teaching a lesson on Daniel in the lions' den. My friend Phil Conrad and I were sitting toward the back, and we weren't paying much attention to the lesson. We were taking turns knuckle-punching each other in the leg. The idea was to make the other guy cry out in pain before you did—no matter how much it hurt. Whoever got the other to say uncle first was the winner.

I had just given Phil a real good shot right above the knee, the kind that makes your whole leg go numb, when I heard Mr. Leatherwood say, "I want some of you to stay after the lesson is over today." Then he started rattling off names.

"Phil Conrad, John Maxwell," he began, and I thought we were in trouble. "Steve Banner and Junior Fowler. Please see me after class." I didn't know what Steve and Junior had done, but I was pretty sure why Phil and I were being called.

After class, he gathered us together. "Come on over here and sit down, boys," he said.

We sat in a semicircle in the corner of our basement classroom and prepared for the worst.

"You boys know that I pray for you and the other boys in class," he started. "Last night as I prayed, I felt God was giving me a word about the four of you."

I breathed a sigh of relief.

"I believe He is calling you into the ministry, and I wanted to be the first one to tell you. He has great things planned for you boys. I also wanted to be the first to lay hands on you and pray for you."

We bowed our heads as he prayed for each of us, placing his hands on our heads. It was incredibly exciting because we all felt as if we got a glimpse of our futures that day. Although I wasn't officially ordained until about 10 years later, I've always considered Glenn Leatherwood's prayer for me that morning to be my official ordination into the ministry. And those other three boys—Steve Banner, Phil Conrad, and Junior Fowler—true to Glenn's word, all became pastors, too.

I consider Glenn Leatherwood to be one of the major influencers in my youth. He not only encouraged me to be a pastor, but he also ministered to me with his kindness and affection during the difficult junior-high years. He made an impact on me in a way my parents couldn't.

I heard recently that Glenn Leatherwood died. I regretted not having heard about it until weeks afterward because I would have liked to return to Ohio for his funeral. It would have given me great pleasure to honor him. Several years ago, I visited him when I was back in Circleville, and I asked him how many children were called into full-time ministry out of his Sunday school classes. He said he wasn't sure about the exact number, but he knew it was at least 30. Obviously, those three boys and I weren't the only ones he influenced.

DON'T TRY TO DO IT ALL YOURSELF

Did you have a Glenn Leatherwood in your life as you were growing up—an adult outside your immediate family who made a significant positive impact on you? Maybe the person influenced you in a way your parents couldn't. It might have been a neighbor, teacher, pastor, or grandparent.

I think that kind of help in parenting was more common in previous generations, especially when more families lived in small communities. People naturally looked out for one another. But today, with people living in larger cities and separated from their relatives, parents seem to be going it alone more and more. But it doesn't have to be that way. Like Margaret and me, you can get the help of others.

THIS CHAPTER IS DEDICATED TO . . .

Those Who Added Value to My Life as a Child

Glenn Leatherwood: He commissioned me into full-time Christian service.

Wayne and Betty McConnaugh: They were like second parents to me. Larry and I were always welcome at their house, and they encouraged our love of sports as our parents couldn't (since they weren't sports people). We watched all the big games at their house. I still remember the 1960 NCAA national championship basketball game between California and Ohio State. We drank Cokes and ate mountains of potato chips as we watched the Buckeyes win.

Charles Conrad (Phil's dad): He always had time for us, and he built the best hideout in the world for Larry, Phil, and me.

Kester and Denise McCain: These lay youth leaders made church the most fun place to be during my high-school years, when a lot of negative influences were trying to attract my attention.

And Those Who Have Added Value to Our Children's Lives

Beth Myers: She became a West Coast grandmother to our children. Elizabeth immediately fell in love with her on our first Holy Land trip. Beth has continued to love her as if she were her own grandchild.

"Uncle" Paul Nanney: He has given Joel Porter the technical education that Margaret and I never could have. Paul has taken him flying, shown him how

to use tools, taught him to do construction and wiring, and worked with him on projects beyond count.

Dick and Debbie Peterson: They have been a second set of parents to our children. Our kids have been theirs, and theirs have been ours. Many times they watched over Elizabeth and Joel when we were on trips. And we know that if anything ever happens to Margaret and me, our children will be in good hands.

Doug and Sherry Bennett: They live halfway across the country in Michigan and hardly know our children, yet they cover them in prayer every day.

Stan and Linda Toler: They have never forgotten the children's birthdays and always send their love with gifts.

Dave Johnson: He has designed the lighting for Skyline Wesleyan Church's living Christmas tree for more than 20 years and has always given Joel Porter his time, mentoring him in every aspect of stage lighting. It's because of his kind attention and expertise that Joel would like someday to run his own lighting company.

Shirley Stauber: She has been a friend not only to Margaret and me, but also to Elizabeth. She takes the time to visit her at her dorm room, bringing her goodies and love.

Miriam Phillips: She has been like a big sister to both kids. She has taken them with her on many trips and given them beautiful experiences.

ENLISTING PEOPLE WHO ADD VALUE

Margaret and I would like some day for you to fill your own dedication page with the names of people who have made a difference for you and your family. You *can* get others to help. People who parent alone are a lot like single parents (who have the hardest job I can think of). They must carry a heavy burden and can't do all they would like to do as parents. If you're a single parent, you know what I'm talking about.

But it doesn't have to be that way. Whether you're a single parent or married, you can and should get help from other people. Occasionally, a person whose influence would benefit your children will come into your life and insist on

> **More often than not, if you want people to help in your children's lives, you'll have to find and enlist them.**

helping you, such as a close friend who loves you. But more often than not, if you want people to help in your children's lives, you'll have to find and enlist them.

Enlisting the help of others does many things:

1. *It extends your influence beyond your home.*
2. *It allows your children to be mentored by experts.*
3. *It develops your children in areas of interest where you may not be able to help.*
4. *It exposes them to other positive points of view.*
5. *It gives them positive models outside the immediate family.*

When you decide *not* to parent alone, a heavy burden lifts from you. You're still responsible for parenting your children, but you no longer have to carry the whole load yourself.

People who will help you influence, teach, and mentor your children can come from nearly anywhere. Here are some ideas about the kinds of people to look for:

Other Christians

An obvious place to seek people who will help you parent your children is your home church. A Sunday school teacher or pastor can touch the life of your child at a crucial time, just as Glenn Leatherwood did with me. And some older children can serve as models to your kids. Their parents might even be good models for you.

Dr. Les Parrott III, a psychologist friend of mine, set up a marriage mentoring program at his home church that shows the value of Christians helping one another. He found established married couples who were willing to spend time with couples in their first year of marriage. The younger husband and wife could ask the older ones questions and get their advice. The established people got an opportunity to pass along what they had learned over the years, and the newlyweds received help during that first year when there are so many adjustments.

The same kind of thing can be done by parents looking for help. Younger parents can look for an older couple whose children have grown up and turned out well. They can ask them questions or get advice as their children reach each stage in their development. Most older couples would be flattered by such a request and pleased to give assistance.

Sometimes the assistance and encouragement come without your even having to ask for them. I've often found that to be true during my many years as a pastor. People would give us words of encouragement at just the right time to keep us going. That was the case when Margaret received a letter from Dennis Suchecki, who is a leader in our church and a good friend. His letter encouraged Margaret for being a good wife, but it also praised her as a parent. He wrote, "You are also a great mother. You're doing such a great job with Elizabeth and Joel! Such different personalities! But you seem to know just how to deal with each of them in a way that is just right."

The children have also received plenty of encouragement. Take a look at this card that Joel Porter received when he was seven years old:

April 21, 1986

Dear Joel Porter,

It was good to see you Sunday night at church service and shake your hand. It made me feel happy inside.

To see you smile and give your hand to touch people with your friendship and welcome them made me very proud of you. You are young now, but you did a big thing (over) →

for me and God.

Seeing your front teeth gone and waiting for your big ones made me think of how you are growing up so much. Just as you have your new teeth being made for you and will soon come in for all to see, I know God is also preparing you and has a very special plan and work for you to do for Him as you grow up.

Meanwhile, you are doing many very special things for Him now --- like shaking people's hands and making them feel good!

Love, Karin William, 125 ♥ 4·21·86   Kar Kard

No parent can do it alone. And no parent should have to. A verse in 2 Timothy talks about pursuing righteousness, but it also contains a phrase about working together that most people miss. It says, "Now flee from youthful lusts, and pursue righteousness, faith, love and peace, *with those who call on the Lord from a pure heart*" (2:22, NASB, emphasis added). God created us to work with one another in a community of believers, to help and be helped by one another.

If you don't have a home church, make it a priority to find one. Look for one that focuses on ministering to families. It should have a strong Sunday school and child-care program, with teachers who love Jesus and children. You'll also want to see if the church plans special days and programs for parents and families. There may be events for Father's Day and Mother's Day, children's church services, family baptisms, and child dedications. Look for activities during the week that cater to children, such as youth activities and AWANA or Pioneer Club. Many parents search for a church based primarily on what it can offer to their children, and there's nothing wrong with that. After all, the church you choose will have a deep influence on their spiritual lives. But also look for a church that will help you grow and become a better parent.

Teachers

After reading breakthrough #4, you may wonder whether I'm against teachers and education. I'm not. I believe in learning, and I support teachers and schools that help children to grow. But I also know that every educational system has both good and bad teachers. If we want our children to be positively affected by the education they receive, we need to make sure they have the best teachers available.

Almost anyone can tell you about a teacher who made a major impact on his or her life. But even as great as that teacher's influence was, I'll bet the teacher wasn't coordinating efforts with the child's parents. The teacher was probably working independently, following his or her own agenda. But think about what could happen if parents and a good teacher partnered together, sharing information that would build on a child's strengths and bolster weaknesses. The positive influence would be multiplied.

Over the years, Margaret and I have spent a good amount of time with Elizabeth's and Joel Porter's teachers. From time to time, we've requested specific teachers for them. And we've always talked to their teachers, to give as well as receive information about the kids.

When Elizabeth was taking gymnastics, she had a coach who knew her sport well enough but tended to discourage rather than encourage Elizabeth. Because Elizabeth's temperament is melancholy-phlegmatic, she sometimes didn't take it well. On several occasions, Margaret (who is a former teacher) went to talk with the coach. Margaret gave her insight into our daughter's personality and asked her to treat Elizabeth more positively. As a result, the coach became more effective with her, and Elizabeth responded well.

I recently talked to a friend who went to his 20-year high-school reunion. While there, he saw the teacher who taught him Spanish when he was a junior and senior. He told her that those Spanish classes had inspired him to study languages in college and become a teaching missionary in South and Central America.

His teacher beamed and said, "Thank you for telling me all those things. You've made my day."

"No, I should thank you," said my friend. "You've made my *life.*"

The more teachers like her that we can put in our children's lives, the more they will be shaped into the people God created them to be.

Extended Family

I was lucky as a kid growing up in Ohio because most of my family lived in that part of the country. We would occasionally visit Grandfather Maxwell in Georgetown, Ohio. And every Thanksgiving, we'd go to his house and see Uncle Millard, Aunt Violet, and their daughter, Phyllis.

But our greatest joy came from our visits to see my mother's family in the suburbs of Detroit. We went there every Christmas, and when we got older, we made fairly regular weekend trips.

Visiting there was like going to a carnival. We spent the whole time playing games and organizing our cousins into sports teams. And in the evenings, we would spend time with Grandmother Roe. She was a warm, loving woman who was very creative. She loved word games. I believe my love for words and my creativity are a legacy from her.

As we grew up and married, for many years my sister, brother, and I continued to live close to one another and our parents. And we did a lot together as adults: anything from vacationing to having dinner, from watching one another's kids to going to church together. We always knew we could count on one another to help out.

In 1981, Margaret and I moved to Southern California, and we went into family withdrawal almost immediately. The first few years, we took a lot of trips back to Ohio because we missed the positive interaction and the value each family member added. Here's an idea of what they provided:

Dad gave *spiritual blessing* to the family.

Mother provided *security*.

Larry lent *wisdom*.

Larry's wife, Anita, created *fun*.

Trish *protected* and *defended* her loved ones.

And Trish's husband, Steve, added great *stability*.

I'm sure you have family members who contribute to your children, too. Spend some time thinking about your family. Identify the ones who can add value to your children or help you to be a better parent. Write their names below, along with the quality you value most in them.

Family Member:	**Quality:**
_____	_____
_____	_____
_____	_____
_____	_____
_____	_____
_____	_____

Don't feel obligated to write the name of every family member on this list. If yours is like 99 percent of all families, you've got relatives you *don't* want influencing your children. Just focus on those who make a positive impact.

Once you've made your list, talk to your children about those relatives and their good qualities. Help the children learn to appreciate them the way you do. Begin thinking of ways to have your children spend time with those family members, too. And point out any positive similarities you see between your children and them. You'll find that children enjoy identifying with an admired relative, especially one you've made into a hero.

> # Children enjoy identifying with an admired relative, especially one you've made into a hero.

Friends

As I work on this book today, my children are not at home. They're off in the mountains, skiing, with our dear friends Dick and Debbie Peterson. That's typical of the kinds of benefits you receive when you share the load of parenting with friends. None of us can do all the things we would like with our children. There aren't enough hours in a day or days in a week. But if you team up with friends whose children are of similar ages and have shared interests, you can help one another. You can take turns driving the kids to soccer practice or softball games. One family can baby-sit for the other to give parents a day off or a night out.

Friends can also mentor your kids in areas outside your expertise. That's what our friend Paul has done with Joel Porter. Paul was a general contractor, though he retired from that business while still in his thirties. Any kind of tool you can name, Paul knows how to use it well. In fact, before each Christmas, we used to ask Paul what tools to get Joel Porter, and then on Christmas Day, Joel had to wait for Paul to come over in the afternoon so he could learn how to use them. I couldn't even identify them, much less work with them.

Paul has been an invaluable mentor to Joel, teaching him how to build all sorts of things over the years. One of Joel's favorite projects was the Christmas star Paul and he built for the roof of the house back when Joel was eight years old. They spent hours buying the wood, measuring and cutting it, fastening it together, and wiring it with lights. Even now, when we put it up each year, I see that it gives Joel great joy, not only because of the sense of accomplishment for having created it, but also because of the wonderful time he and Paul had putting it together.

As you think about your friends and how they can add value to the lives of your children, remember that it's important to always get to know the people and build relationships with them first. Any help you get and give should grow out of your friendship with them. You never want to befriend people just so you can use them to help your children. You also want to learn about their character before putting them with your kids. No skill or help is worth the damage that can be done by exposing your children to a person of questionable character.

People with Special Gifts

Sometimes your children have needs that require you to look outside your family or circle of friends. In the case of Joel Porter, if we hadn't been fortunate enough to have Paul as a friend, we would have had to look for someone to give Joel the technical and mechanical training he desired.

That's what my parents did for my siblings and me as we were growing up. For example, since I needed a piano teacher and neither of my parents played, they asked Wayne Reno to teach me. He was a wonderful music teacher who was also a godly man. After each lesson, he talked to me about God and how He loved me. I used to think he did that out of kindness and compassion, but now I'm not sure. I just received a letter from his son that said Wayne considered me the orneriest student he ever had! Now I have a suspicion that he talked to me about God because he thought I was headed for hell!

My parents enlisted the aid of people with special gifts for Larry, too. Kester McCain, who I mentioned was a youth leader at our church, owned an aluminum siding and awning business. He was a hard worker, a good Christian, and a sharp businessman. Dad arranged for Larry to work with Kester, and from the time Larry was in junior high until he graduated from high school, he helped Kester install siding and hang awnings.

It's hard to measure the impact Kester had on Larry. But I think Larry received encouragement and mentoring in the area of business at a time when he needed them most. I believe that boost is partly responsible for Larry's success today.

No matter how good a parent you are, you shouldn't parent alone. Other people can help you, but you have to look for them. Begin with your immediate and then extended family. Ask the help of friends. Seek out mentors and models in the church. Remember, always look first for good character, and then for skills and availability.

And while you're looking, make it a goal to find others *you* can help. As members of the Body of Christ, we're to be givers, too, not just receivers. Think about how you can add value to the children of family members, friends, and other Christians at church. Develop relationships and then partnerships. There's no reason you—or they—should have to parent alone.

Breakthrough #6

The Growth That Counts
Isn't in Years

The potential breakthrough for the parent . . .
the development of a growth game plan

The potential breakthrough for the child . . .
maturity

An extra-large man stepped on a public scale, not knowing it was out of order. He dropped a coin into the slot, and the indicator on the scale bounced its way up and stopped at 75 pounds. As he did that, a little boy and his mother walked by on the sidewalk. The boy, seeing the scale stopped at 75 pounds, shouted out, "Look, Mom! That man is hollow!"

Hollow is a word that, unfortunately, describes many children growing up today. On the outside, they look fine. As they get older, they get taller and fill out. Their bodies mature until they become young adults. But they may not be growing on the inside; they may not be experiencing personal growth, and that's the growth that really counts.

GROWTH IS NOT AUTOMATIC

Personal growth doesn't come simply with the passing of years. Chuck Swindoll said:

> There is an enormous difference between growing old in the Lord and growing up in Him. One is automatic and requires no effort at all . . . just aging. But the other is never automatic, or easy. It calls for personal discipline, continual determination, and spiritual desire. Churches are full of sleepy saints who are merely logging time in God's family.

Though he was speaking primarily of spiritual growth, the same is true of any kind of personal growth—it's not automatic but instead requires discipline, determination, and desire.

I heard of a teacher whose ambition was to become a school administrator. She spent her first year adapting to her new teaching job, and then she settled into a regular routine. After working several years, she felt she had put in enough time to begin looking for a principal's job.

Each year, she applied for every opening for a principal in her district. And every year, she failed to get a position. After 15 years of teaching and more than eight years of applying, she was exasperated. The final straw came when a teacher she knew had been teaching for only seven years got a position for which she had applied.

Angrily, she called the superintendent. "I can't believe you hired her over me," she railed. "I have seniority. I have 15 years of experience to her seven!"

"No, you're mistaken," the superintendent told her. "She has seven years of experience. You have one year of experience—repeated 15 times."

YOU'RE ONLY YOUNG ONCE, BUT YOU CAN BE IMMATURE INDEFINITELY

People who fail to pursue personal growth never reach their potential. Often they don't even reach full maturity as people. Maturity comes not with age but with the acceptance of responsibility. Abigail Van Buren, in one of her "Dear Abby" columns, once said maturity meant:

> To be able to stick with a job until it is finished;
> To do a job well without being supervised;
> To be able to carry money without spending it;
> To bear an injustice without trying to get even.

Many people today embody qualities directly opposite the ones described by Mrs. Van Buren. They seem to have trouble staying with one job for any period of time. Left unsupervised, they don't do any work at all, much less do a job to the best of their ability. When it comes to money, most of the people in our society spend not only what they carry, but also money they haven't earned yet—by using credit cards. And bearing an injustice is the last thing anyone wants to do. The courts are filled with people trying to get what's

> **Maturity comes not with age but with the acceptance of responsibility.**

coming to them and—when possible—whatever they can get even when it's undeserved.

The trend today is toward immaturity—mental, emotional, and spiritual. I believe the root of that trend is lack of growth.

WHY PEOPLE FAIL TO GROW

People fail to grow for many reasons. Here are the four most common ones I've observed:

- *Busyness:* There's a saying I've heard recently; maybe you've heard it, too: "God put me on earth to accomplish a certain number of things. Right now I'm so far behind that I will never die!" That's the way many people feel today—overworked and overwhelmed. And that's their excuse for not growing personally. But the truth is that we all make time for what's important to us.

- *Laziness:* Deep down in each of us is a desire not to work, and making growth a priority is work. It takes effort. But it does have its rewards. As Teddy Roosevelt said, "There has never yet been a person in our history who led a life of ease whose name is worth remembering."

- *Lack of desire:* I meet a lot of people who express no desire to grow. They've reached a certain milestone or destination in their lives, and they think they've arrived. That milestone can be the completion of a degree, the attainment of a certain job, a marriage, parenthood, or the achievement of a certain salary. But people who think that way have what I call "destination disease." They don't place enough value on personal growth, and as a result, they will never reach their potential. Milestones are just markers; only growth releases potential.

- *No plan for growth:* Finally, people don't grow because they have no plan to do it. Many times, they don't realize they won't experience growth unless they pursue it. Other times, they have no plan because they don't know how to go about constructing one.

SIGNPOSTS ON THE ROAD OF PERSONAL GROWTH

Although I'm best known around the country for my books and seminars on leadership, if I were to identify a theme that has been a part of my life from childhood to the present, it would be the desire for growth. It has been a constant and a catalyst for me.

Specifically, three major factors have influenced me in this area:

A Lifestyle of Personal Growth

The whole process started for me at home when I was a kid. My father believed in personal growth. He practiced it, and he planned it for us kids. At the core of his desire for us was his allowance plan, which I later realized was revolutionary. He always said, "If you want to raise a garbage man, pay your child an allowance to take out the garbage. If you want your child to be a great man or woman of God, pay your child to read good books."

I can't remember a time when my siblings and I weren't on a growth plan. When we were little, Mom and Dad read to us constantly. As we got older, we read a lot ourselves. At each stage of our development as readers, they introduced us to new books.

By the time I was in the third grade, I was required to read for 30 minutes every day (in addition to my quiet time and any reading for school). At first, a lot of my reading was of Bible stories. But as I grew, Mom and Dad gave me other books to read, such as *The Power of Positive Thinking,* by Norman Vincent Peale, and *How to Win Friends and Influence People,* by Dale Carnegie. They picked the books, and they paid me my allowance to read them.

Each night at dinner, during our family time, we discussed our reading. Mom and Dad would ask us questions, and we would tell them what we had read. We were also encouraged to state our opinions. It was an effective way to process and apply the material. As we got older, we were allowed to pick some of our own books to read, with Dad's approval of them. Helping to plan our own growth gave us additional incentive to read and learn.

I participated in Dad's growth-for-allowance plan every weekday until I graduated from high school. That means I read for 30 minutes a day, five days a week, for more than 10 years. It developed a tremendous desire and discipline for growth to the point that it became a lifestyle. And it also made me realize that nothing in life brings more happiness than personal growth.

A Strategy for Personal Growth

In 1974, I reached a second personal-growth milestone. At that time, I had been a pastor for about five years, and I was successful. In my first church, we had grown from a first-Sunday attendance of three to an average attendance of more than 200. We had even set a record attendance of 301—and that in a sparsely populated rural community. In 1974, I was in my second pastorate, this time in a church that was once again growing after being on an attendance plateau for nearly a decade. It was a joyous time: People were getting saved, and our church was recognized one year as having the fastest-growing Sunday school in all of Ohio.

In that year, I met Kurt Kampmeier, a man who changed my life. I had lunch with him one day, and he showed me a plan for personal growth that he was selling for $795. That was a lot of money back then—5 percent of the $14,800 I earned as a pastor that year! But I realized that even if we had trouble affording it, I couldn't afford *not* to get it for the sake of my personal growth.

I went home that evening and told Margaret about it. She recognized its value immediately. "John," she said, "you need to get this plan no matter how much it costs. Let's figure out how to make it work." We sat down that night and figured out what we could cut from our budget and what meals we would skip for the next six months so we could pay for it. And the next morning, I wrote Kurt Kampmeier a check for $795.

The growth plan helped me to develop that year, but it also had greater, long-lasting effects on me. First, it made me realize that if I wanted to continue to grow, I had to be strategic about it. For the best results, I had to have a plan. Second, it made me realize that growth always comes at a price—in terms of money, time, and discipline. These are truths I have now embraced for more than 20 years.

From that time on, I put myself on a deliberate and strategic personal plan for growth. I subscribe to several tape services and listen to cassettes each month. I take more than a dozen periodicals, which I read and use as resources for my filing system. And every year, I identify books that I will read, particularly ones on leadership. All that has made a huge difference in my life.

Horace Greeley once said of Abraham Lincoln, "There was probably no year of his life when he was not a wiser, cooler, and better man than he had been the year preceding." That's an incredible goal that each of us should strive for. And a strategic plan for personal growth helps to make that goal attainable.

The Production of a Personal-Growth Plan

In 1993, I experienced a third personal-growth milestone. I was teaching a leadership seminar in Kansas City, Missouri, and I was talking about how I have my children read books and listen to tapes, much as my father did with me. All of a sudden, I had a flash of insight. I realized the people I was talking to had no such plan for their lives. I was so convinced of this that I said to the group of 300 people, "If anyone here has put himself on a plan for personal growth, come up to me during the break and tell me about it." No one came forward.

At the next conference, I made the same announcement, and once again, no one came up to tell me about a plan for growth. Over the course of several months, I must have asked more than 1,000 people if they had a plan, and not one person responded positively.

That's when I decided I needed to help people plan their growth. In 1994, I introduced a one-year personal-growth plan for leaders. The plan describes a strategy for growth, and it has the materials they need for a whole year. It includes a weekly devotional, weekly leadership-equipping cassettes, and the best 12 books available on leadership—one for every month of the year. Here's the pattern I suggest they use:

Monday	*one hour using the* One Hour with God *devotional*
Tuesday	*one hour listening to a leadership tape*
Wednesday	*one hour selecting and filing highlights from the leadership tape*

Thursday	*one hour reading the month's leadership book*
Friday	*$1/2$ hour reading the leadership book*
	$1/2$ hour filing from the book, reflecting, and applying concepts

I've found that this system works well for most people, and they often see quick growth in their ability to lead.

As I mentioned, I've found few pastors who have put themselves on a personal growth plan, and most parents are the same. Neither they nor their children are on a strategic growth plan. That's one reason I want to show you how to prepare a plan for your children. It will develop your children's potential and help your whole family.

LAYING A FOUNDATION FOR FAMILY GROWTH

Before I explain how to develop a plan for your children, allow me to show you how to build a strong foundation for your family's growth. Follow these eight principles and you'll be in a position to set your family on the right path.

Start with Yourself

Several years ago, I visited Westminster Abbey in England. On the crypt of an Anglican bishop who died around the year 1100 were these words:

> When I was young and free and my imagination had no limits, I dreamed of changing the world. As I grew older and wiser, I discovered the world would not change, so I shortened my sights somewhat and decided to change only my country. But it, too, seemed immovable.
>
> As I grew into my twilight years, in one last desperate attempt, I settled for changing only my family, those closest to me, but alas, they would have not of it.
>
> And now as I lie on my deathbed, I suddenly realize: If I had only changed myself first, then by example I would have changed my family. From their inspiration and encouragement, I would then have been able to better my country and, who

knows, I may have even changed the world.

When I talk to pastors around the country who want to grow their churches, I tell them, "If you want to change the church, change the pastor."

When I talk to business-people, I tell them, "Change the leader—change the organization." And now I'll tell you that the same is true for families. If you want to change the children,

> **If you want to change the children, change the parent. Any growth plan for your family must begin with you.**

change the parent. Any growth plan for your family must begin with you.

Ask the Important Questions

E. Stanley Jones said, "The chief way you and I are disloyal to Christ is when we make small what he intended to make large." That's what we do to our children when we aren't dedicated to helping ourselves and them grow. Check your level of commitment by asking yourself:

Do I believe *I* have the potential to grow?	Yes	No
Do I believe *my family* has growth potential?	Yes	No
Do I have a *desire* for my family to grow?	Yes	No
Can I *do something* to promote the family's growth?	Yes	No
Am I *willing to do whatever it takes* for them to grow?	Yes	No

If your answer to any of these questions is no, you'll have to resolve that issue before you can develop your family's growth potential.

Get Rid of Excuses

An English proverb says, "One of these days means none of these days." You may have an excuse for not growing. You may be waiting for inspiration, permission, money, time, a deadline, a relationship, approval, or authority. If you continue to *wait*, you'll *continue* to wait. Only one thing can get you started—you!

Make a Decision to Change

We don't decide whether we will be people. But we do choose whether we will be ignorant, undeveloped people or people who have sought to reach our maximum potential. Growth means change. If we're not willing to change, we won't be able to grow.

See the Big Picture

People in our society seem to be fixated on what they can get. Nearly everyone wants to know what's in it for him. However, the purpose of personal growth is not what we *get* for it but what we *become* by it.

Before James Garfield became president of the United States, he was the head of Hiram Institute, a private school. And it is said that a father once asked him if he couldn't shorten the course of study for his son, possibly from four years down to two.

"Certainly," Garfield is said to have replied. "But it all depends upon what you want to make of your boy. When God wants to make an oak tree, he takes a hundred years. When he wants to make a squash, he requires only two months."

The big picture is that personal growth is for the long haul, not an immediate return. When you begin developing yourself and your family, it's possible that you may see positive results in a few months. But it's also possible that you won't see results for a decade. And if that's the way it is, don't despair and don't take shortcuts. "Do not be afraid of going slowly," says a Chinese proverb. "Be afraid of standing still." Remember, your goal is to affect your children for eternity, and that has a way of putting things into perspective.

Make the Home a Growth Environment

If you want your children to grow, create a hothouse climate where they will flourish. A growth environment is a place where . . .

- Others are ahead of them.
- They're continually challenged.
- The focus is forward.
- The atmosphere is affirming.

- They are asked to get out of their comfort zone.
- They wake up excited.
- They need not fear failure.
- Others are growing.
- There's a willingness to change.
- Growth is modeled and expected.

Children can't provide their own positive environment. Their parents must create it for them.

Be a Positive Learner

How far we progress in the learning process is determined by our attitude. When a negative person makes a mistake, he withdraws and becomes cynical. But a positive person can turn errors, false starts, or fumbles into learning experiences. As Allen H. Neuharth, founder of *USA Today*, said, "Don't just learn something from every experience; learn something positive."

Give Up to Grow Up

As I mentioned earlier, I learned that any kind of growth has a cost associated with it. You can't hold on to what you have with both hands and still grab hold of something new. You must let go of the old to embrace the new. Or as Ralph Waldo Emerson said it, "For everything you gain, you give up something." Be willing to make sacrifices in order to grow.

HOW TO DEVELOP A GROWTH PLAN FOR YOUR CHILDREN

Once you've got the right attitude and environment, you're ready to get started. Here are five steps that will help you develop a growth plan for your children:

1. Assess Your Child's Needs

The process begins with assessing your child's needs. Think about the answers to the following questions for each child:

What is my child's age? Younger children will have to be read to or shown videos. As they get older, your choices for material will increase. Always use age-appropriate materials so children don't get discouraged by overly difficult reading.

What is my child's bent? Whenever possible, use material that takes advantage of your child's bent. And focus your plan on the child's method of learning—by listening, watching, or doing. In the case of our kids, Elizabeth learns best by listening, so we gave her a lot of tapes. Joel Porter, on the other hand, learns best by doing, so we have constantly given him projects to do.

What are my child's top three interests? One of the best ways to motivate children is to offer them an opportunity to learn in their areas of interest. If your child likes trains, for instance, and you want to teach him about character, look for train stories that have a strong moral message. Or take him to a train museum as a reward for using good manners. And while you're there, use whatever you can find in the museum to teach positive lessons.

What are my child's top three spiritual gifts? It's never too early to start encouraging your child to develop her spiritual gifts. If you don't know what those gifts are, buy a gifts test from your local Christian bookstore (or order one from INJOY; see details on how at the back of this book). If your child is a teenager, ask him to take the test. If your child is younger, take the test for her, answering the questions based on your observations.

What is my child's greatest need? Over the course of your child's growing-up years, you'll want to spend time focusing on several areas of need, such as spiritual development, character, relationships, attitude, and spiritual gifts. But at different times, a child will need particular attention in an area—just as Joel Porter did in the area of honesty at one point.

What is my child's greatest weakness? Try to be honest and fair concerning your child's weaknesses, neither ignoring them nor finding fault in too many areas.

Now that you've thought about each question, write your answers below:

MY CHILD'S NEEDS

What is my child's age? _____

What is my child's bent? _____

What are my child's top three interests?

_____

_____

_____

What are my child's top three spiritual gifts?

_____

_____

_____

What is my child's greatest need?

_____

What is my child's greatest weakness?

_____

2. Determine Where to Focus the Growth

Now that you've answered the questions, you'll probably begin seeing some of the areas where you'll want to focus your attention. As you do, keep in mind that you'll want to work in two ways. First, you'll want to concentrate primarily on building your child's strengths. The greatest leaders and achievers in history developed their strengths until they reached their potential. Then they were able to make an extraordinary contribution.

Second, you'll need to shore up the weaknesses. Any time you see a weakness that can cause your child long-term harm, you need to make it a target of growth, especially if it's in the area of character. No matter how well you try to build on strengths, if serious weaknesses aren't addressed, there will come a fall. Just look at the lives of people like Jim Bakker and Jimmy Swaggart if you have any doubts.

3. Find Resources

When children are young, you can choose material that isn't highly focused on a single area of growth. Character and biblical literacy are the best areas for growth. Show them well-done Bible videos, and read them Bible stories and selections from books such as William Bennett's *Book of Virtues.* When Elizabeth and Joel Porter were small, we used *Fun Ideas for Family Devotions,* by Ginger Jurries and Karen Mulder, and material prepared by Walk Thru the Bible. Another favorite was *The Bible in Pictures for Little Eyes*, a wonderful Bible storybook that reminded Margaret of the lessons her Grandmother Porter used to teach her in Sunday school when she was a little girl.

> **Under normal circumstances, you should spend at least twice as much time building on strengths as you do correcting weaknesses.**

As your children get older, you'll need to become more strategic. Take a look at your answers from the questions above, and pick the top two or three areas to work on during the next three months. Under normal circumstances, you should spend at least twice as much time building on strengths as you do correcting weaknesses.

Your next step will be to go to a Christian bookstore (or your church's library). Ask for the help of the manager or the person who knows children's books, and tell him or her you want to see the best books on the subjects you've picked in the age ranges of your children. Look through the books, and pick out the ones that would be of benefit and interest to your children.

4. Design a Plan for Growth

Once you've selected the books you want your children to read during the coming three months, chart each one's growth plan on a grid like that provided. Remember that each child will have 2¹/₂ hours to read every week, and the plan should be based on his or her reading rate. It's usually wise to have children read one book at a time until it's finished rather than jump from book to book. They'll be better able to remember what they're reading, and they'll experience a sense of accomplishment when they've finished a book.

This Quarter's Plan for Growth
Reading 30 minutes each day helps you grow to reach your potential!

Week	Monday	Tuesday	Wednesday	Thursday	Friday	Sat./Sun.
1						Off
2						Off
3						Off
4						Off
5						Off
6						Off
7						Off
8						Off
9						Off
10						Off
11						Off
12						Off
13						Off

This month's book(s):

_____   _____
_____   _____
_____   _____
_____   _____

5. Set Aside Daily Growing Time

Once you've designed their growth plan, you won't be able to just turn your children loose to complete it. In the beginning, you'll have to help them with the daily discipline of getting it done. Start by designating a time and place for them to read each day. It will have to be a quiet place where no television or radio can distract them. You may even want to use that time for your own personal growth.

Over the years, Margaret and I have usually asked Elizabeth and Joel Porter to read for 30 minutes each day, but we've also given them tapes to listen to. They've been pretty good about sticking with it, but we've also given them incentives—we've paid them. At different times, we've used a number of systems. The simplest plan has been to have a weekly allowance that they receive only if they do their reading. (They're also required to do their chores around the house and receive no allowance or pay for those tasks.)

Sometimes we created a point system for them to earn money during the summer. We'd make a book-audiotape-and-project list and assign a point value to each item. They could earn points by reading a book, listening to a tape and writing a one-page report on it, or completing a project. And then we'd pay them according to the points they earned.

In recent years, we've had a standing offer to them so they could earn extra money. If they listened to an INJOY Life Club tape (the ones I create for Christian leaders each month) and wrote a one-page typed report on it, they earned $10.

This personal-growth system really works with kids, but it doesn't work if you don't get them to read. During the summers following third and fourth grade for Elizabeth and Joel Porter, we let them read nearly anything and paid them for the number of books they read. It's at that time that reading really accelerates, and we wanted them to develop a love for books and reading during those impressionable years.

I believe Margaret and I are now beginning to see some positive results from the growth plan Elizabeth and Joel Porter have been following. But only the passage of time will give us a full picture of its impact. In many ways, it's easier to measure the impact my father had on me, my brother, and my sister.

A couple of years ago, I received a letter from a pastor friend who is a superintendent in the Wesleyan church. His name is O. W. Willis, and he had just finished a camp meeting with my dad, who had preached there. Here's part of what O. W. wrote:

As I felt his spirit and worked with him [Dad], the thought came to me of how the Lord has used your life. But forever as long as you minister, regardless of how high the Lord takes you, I am sure that you will realize and recognize you will forever be standing on the shoulders of your dear dad.

When I think back on all my father has done for me—not the least of which was putting me on a plan for personal growth and modeling it himself every day—I recognize that all I've achieved has, indeed, come as the result of my standing on his shoulders.

Margaret's and my desire has been to allow Elizabeth and Joel Porter to do the same—to stand on our shoulders. And you can do the same with your children. Don't worry if you've gotten a late start in your journey to personal growth. No matter what you've done—or haven't done—you can help your children climb a bit higher than you do.

Make your own shoulders as broad as you can by putting yourself on a plan for growth and continuing with it. And then help your children climb by exposing them to the influential books you've read. It may be the soundest investment you'll ever make in your children's future.

Breakthrough #7

Do Everything Possible
to Influence the Influencers
in Your Child's Life

The potential breakthrough for the parent . . .
continued positive influence

The potential breakthrough for the child . . .
continued positive direction

When I was about 10 years old, Larry and I discovered the local canteen. We had heard about it from our friends at school, and it sounded like the most wonderful place in the world. It had pinball machines, pool tables, a soda fountain—everything we thought we could ever want.

Several places in town were off limits to us, and we knew the canteen was on the list. Some of the tough kids from bad families hung out there, and occasionally there were fights. But those facts only added to its allure. We really wanted to go, and being a positive thinker even then, I figured Larry and I could talk Dad into letting us go. When we approached him, he said, "Boys, let's go down there and take a look at the place."

When we first walked in, Larry and I were a little embarrassed. After all, nobody else had his dad there with him. But we got over it quickly. We walked around looking at all the great stuff. Dad took in the scene and asked, "Boys, what is it you like about this place?"

We walked him over to the pool tables and showed them to him.

"All right, what else?" he asked.

We showed him the pinball machine and other things we liked.

"Okay, boys," he said finally, "let's go home."

The next day at dinner, Dad made an announcement. "I want you boys to know that your mother and I bought a pool table today," he said. "It's going to be delivered in about a week. Larry, you and Johnny will need to clean the basement this Saturday and get it ready."

We couldn't believe it. And we were even more excited several weeks later when a pinball machine was also delivered! Soon after that, we got a Ping-Pong table, too! We put a light over the pool table, hung some signs on the walls, and in a matter of a few weeks, our cellar became the Basement Canteen. The allure of the canteen in town quickly faded away, and our house became *the* place to be for us and our friends.

Before long, we always seemed to have a big group of kids at our house. Mom likes to tell a story about Grandpa Maxwell, who came to visit us about six months after we created the Basement Canteen. Mom was in the kitchen, preparing lunch, and a group of us were playing out in the yard. Grandpa Maxwell came into the kitchen, and she could see he was agitated. He said, "Laura, do you know how many boys there are in your backyard?"

"Yes," she replied. "There are 13—and I know the name of every one of them."

"How can you stand all that racket?" he said. "Listen to them. They're so noisy!"

"Yes, they are," Mom said. "But at least my boys are in my backyard. I know where they are and who they're with."

My parents wanted to continue having a positive influence on us as we grew up, and they found a terrific way to do it. At the same time, they directed us away from many negative influences. Providing us with the Basement Canteen wasn't easy for them financially, though I didn't realize it at the time. Mom and Dad went without some things to do it. For example, Dad had only one good pair of shoes and one good suit, and our vacations were always family outings in the car— usually to visit relatives. Dad was a good money manager, and he and Mom made careful choices based on priorities that put the family first.

WHEN INFLUENCE TAKES A U-TURN

Their actions reflected a lot of wisdom. They showed that they understood how influences change during the course of a child's life.

When children are young, their parents hold the most important place in their lives. I'm reminded of a story about a six-year-old girl who was performing during her church's children's department program. Standing before the congregation, she completely forgot her Bible verse. Her mother, seated in the front row, mouthed the words of Jesus: "I am the light of the world." The girl relaxed and radiated confidence. In a voice like a cheerleader's, she proudly called out, "My mother is the light of the world."

But when children get older, as their parents' influence decreases, their peers' influence increases. And the direction children take is likely to be a U-turn.

INFLUENCERS

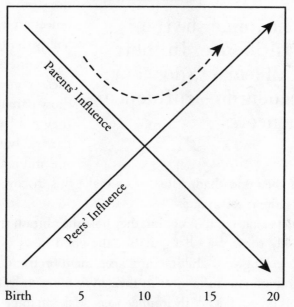

As a result, parents become less like the mother of the little girl in the church program and more like the father who said:

> I'm paid to be a foreman.
> My job is leading men.
> My boss thinks I'm a natural,
> But if I am, why then,
> I wish someone would tell me
> Why snow-swept walks I clean,
> When in the house sit two grown sons
> Who made the football team.

INFLUENCING THE INFLUENCERS

When I teach leadership at conferences around the country, I always explain that leadership is influence. Most people misunderstand leadership. They think it's based on position. But positional leadership is the weakest and most basic form. Real leadership—the kind that transcends position and functions in any type of organization or situation—is a reflection of the leader's ability to *influence* others.

> If you can no longer be the dominant influencer in their lives, you can learn to do what effective leaders do—influence their influencers.

I mention this because there comes a point in most parents' lives when they still have the title of parent, but they've lost the influence over their children that they once had. Most of us make this discovery some time during our children's teen years.

When many parents reach this point, they hold their breath and hope everything eventually turns out all right. But the good news is that you can continue influencing your children and keep them on track. If you can no longer be the dominant influencer in their lives, you can learn to do what effective leaders do—influence their influencers. Make an impact on your kids through the places they go and the people with whom they spend their time.

PLACES OF INFLUENCE

Looking at some of the key places where your children spend time may help you get a handle on some of the influences in their lives. Here are the top five:

Home

At least until their teen years, children spend the most time at home, so it's important to use the home to influence the influencers in their lives. As I mentioned, my parents always tried to make our home attractive to us and our friends. That way, they could keep an eye on us and help us understand those other kids.

For example, Mom always talked to us about the kids we had coming over to visit. I remember one time when I was in the third grade, I was out playing baseball in the backyard with Larry and a couple of his friends. When one of his friends—I'll call him Bill—had a ground ball bounce up and hit him in the chin, he cussed. Later that evening, after the other boys had gone home and Larry and I were cleaning up to get ready for dinner, Mom talked to us about Bill.

"Larry, John, the new boy who was with you today—Bill—have you known him long?" she asked.

"We met him when school started."

"So he goes to your school then?"

"Yes, ma'am."

"School's only been going for a month, so I guess you haven't known him very long."

"No. We started hanging out with him at recess a couple of weeks ago."

"Tell me about Bill."

"Well, he's a friend of Jim's. He moved to town from Indiana during the summer. He likes to play baseball, and his dad works in an office downtown."

"That's good, Honey. I noticed while you were playing ball he used some bad language. Does he always talk like that?"

"No. Well, maybe sometimes. But only when he gets real mad."

"Does he get mad a lot?"

"Yeah, kind of."

"Do you boys remember what the Bible says about that kind of talk?"

"Yes," Larry said. "It says, 'Let there be no filthiness, nor silly talk, nor levity, which are not fitting; but instead let there be thanksgiving.'" (We memorized a lot of Scripture as kids.)

"I want you to be nice to Bill and let Jesus' light shine through you," she said. "But I think it would be a good idea if you didn't spend too much time with him. I don't want you boys to start talking that way. Birds of a feather flock together."

Mom talked to us like that about our friends all the time, about the good things as well as the bad. We were often allowed to invite friends over to dinner, and they were brought into our family conversations. From the time we were small, my parents helped us learn which qualities to look for in our friends. They wanted us to love everyone, but they wanted us to be *close* to people who would be positive influences.

Another way my parents influenced us was by exposing us regularly to interesting people. Whereas other parents might send their children to bed early when a special guest came to their home, my parents included us in those visits. We were allowed to take part in the conversation, but of course, we had to behave and use good manners.

Interesting people were always coming to dinner or visiting my parents. I remember that Trish was particularly influenced by Mary Johnson, a missionary to India. She was well known for continually asking the question, "What would Jesus do?" My favorite visitor was John Kunkle, a missionary to South America. We used to call him Uncle Kunkle. Wherever he traveled, he took along a beautiful macaw who talked. And every time he visited us, he let me play with the bird. Uncle Kunkle was a good example to me of how much fun a person could have while serving God with all his heart.

Because the people who visit you can have such a lasting impact on your children, think twice about potential visitors to your home. If you *must* spend time with someone negative, invite him to the office or out to a restaurant, and leave your children at home. On the other hand, take the initiative to have interesting people visit your home. For example, the next time foreign missionaries you know need a place to stay while in town, volunteer to put them up. Or ask them to dinner. Invite other strong Christians you know to visit.

I'll bet that right now you could list at least five interesting people you know whom you could invite over for dinner or a social activity. Think about it, and determine to have at least one person over to your house each month for fellowship—and for the good of your children.

School

Your children spend the next-largest amount of time at school. Since I talked about that relationship in breakthrough #5, I don't need to say much more here. But your children's teachers are strong influences in their lives.

Margaret and I have sent Elizabeth and Joel to private Christian schools. I don't think the education they've received there is necessarily better (or worse) than they would have gotten in public school. We believe the greatest asset of a Christian school is that the people in authority share our fundamental values. But if your children are in public school, it's possible to achieve similar results. Get to know the teachers, request those whose values are similar to yours, and develop a relationship of cooperation with them.

Church

As I also suggested before, choose a church based not primarily on your own needs, but more on the needs of your children. And think ahead to the future. Even if you have a child who is only in fourth grade, check the youth program at the church. Once your child has developed relationships at the church, you won't want to change churches when she turns 13 in order to find a good junior-high program.

Places Where They Want to Go

Your children will undoubtedly find other places they want to go, just as Larry and I did with the local canteen. Check out the places before you make decisions. I remember when I was in junior high school, I decided I wanted to learn to bowl. My parents always encouraged me to try new things, so they were supportive, but they didn't give me permission right away.

"John," said my dad, "I want to take a look at those bowling alleys first. I'll let you know on Friday if you can go."

I was eager to go and wanted to know right away, but I knew that wasn't an option. Besides, I knew that if my dad said he'd tell me on Friday, he would tell me on Friday. Sure enough, Friday evening came around, and at dinner he told me I could go to one of the two bowling alleys in town but not the other. And the next day I did.

Years later, I figured out what had made the difference to my dad. The one that was off limits served alcohol, and Dad felt it didn't have the kind of family atmosphere he wanted for us.

As your children ask to go other places, check them out. Certainly, let them go to the places that will be good for them. And when they want to go somewhere you think they don't belong, hold your ground but offer alternatives. Sometimes there will be another place of the same kind available—a second bowling alley. Other times, you can offer an alternative at home. In the end, that's one of the best strategies. Make home so attractive that they'd rather be there than some of those other places.

Places Where You Want Them to Go

Finally, you will want to introduce your children to some places of influence that they wouldn't seek on their own:

Church activities. Be on the lookout for fun activities sponsored by your church: movies, all-night lock-ins, mission trips, and so on. The more your kids are influenced by other Christians with the same values, the better. And here's something for you to think about: When most parents discipline their children, they take away church activities as well as other privileges. But I recommend you not do that. Margaret and I have always wanted our children to receive the benefit of that positive influence no matter what. So even when punished, they were allowed to go to church. I believe that has been a good choice for us and our children, and I think it would be for you, too.

Christian concerts and theater. Many cities have Christian theater groups that put on excellent productions. And sometimes Christian musical artists hold concerts in a local arena or auditorium. Take your children to those events. Show them there's more available to them than secular entertainment.

Christian camp. Seek out a Christian camp for your children. You never can tell how strong an influence it can have on them. I should know—Marsha Watson introduced me to a girl named Margaret Porter at camp. Now people know her as Margaret Maxwell. By sending me to camp, my parents put me in the place where I met the most influential person in my life!

We've sent Elizabeth and Joel to camp many years. It has always been a good experience for them. It's given them a break from us (and vice versa), and it has exposed them to positive Christian teaching and role models in a fun setting.

After the kids have returned home from camp, I've asked them to write about the experience. Here's what Joel Porter wrote when he was 11 or 12 years old:

> Camp was fun to go to, but the most fun was being with friends. . . . It was fun to have all that fun and games, but the most fun was playing basketball. . . . I liked the second to last breakfast. It was French toast, sausage, and biscuits. [You can tell he's my son.] The best night was Thursday. It was when 42 people went up to the altar and recommitted their lives or became a Christian. That was the most fun of all.

It touched my heart that he thought the best night was the one where so many children became Christians.

If you haven't already been sending your children to camp, look for one. Ask Christian friends or your pastor to recommend a camp in your area. Your church may sponsor groups each summer. Explore the possibilities. Lots of kids get saved at camp; that may be where your son or daughter meets Jesus.

PEOPLE OF INFLUENCE

You can see that people are influential in our children's lives. That's why it's important to do three things in respect to the relationships our children have.

Know the Background of the Influencers

You can't take for granted that all the people your children meet and want to spend time with come from healthy backgrounds. Drug use and alcohol consumption continue to be on the rise, as do abuse and domestic violence, and children are the ones who suffer most as a result. You can find out a lot about the children your kids spend time with by talking to them and to your kids about them. You don't want to become an FBI agent, but you do want to know what kinds of influences you're dealing with.

Know Their Level of Influence

If you observe any group of children for a length of time, you'll notice that there are leaders and followers. There's a definite pecking order. Some are the influencers, and others are the influenced. You need to know whether your children are leaders or followers.

Elizabeth and Joel Porter are very different from each other in this respect. Elizabeth's natural inclination is to follow rather than lead. She doesn't like to make decisions, and she likes to think things through before acting. As a result, the people she spends her time with have always been a concern to us, especially during the teenage years, when she was going through a time of questioning about her values and goals.

Joel Porter, on the other hand, has a strong personality. Margaret and I used to say, "He'll lead people either to hell or to heaven, but one thing's for certain—wherever he goes, he'll be leading." We know he's more likely to influence others than to be influenced by them. And we've worked hard to keep positive influences and goals in front of him to keep him on track.

Watch your children as they interact with others to get an idea of their level of influence. And keep in mind that the more inclined they are to follow, the more you'll need to be concerned about the company they keep.

Give Special Attention to Critical Relationships

While your children are in their formative years, many people will influence them. Most children spend a lot of time with the person they consider to be their best friend, so you'll want to be sure the character and family background of that friend are strong. But by far the greatest influences in children's lives are the people they date. Any dating relationship is a potential marriage relationship, and a marriage partner does more to make or break a person than any other relationship this side of heaven.

As I mentioned before, from the time Larry, Trish, and I were little, Mom and Dad talked to us about what to look for in a mate, and sometimes we prayed for our then-unknown future spouses. When we didn't date people who would make the most ideal marriage partners, Mom and Dad didn't try to break up the relationship, but they didn't encourage it, either. And as I found out later, Mom prayed those negative influencers out of our lives.

When I began dating Margaret, I could tell immediately that my parents liked her because they were always positive when they saw her. But as she and I got a little more serious in our relationship, there was a sudden change in how my parents reacted to her—they actually became *more* encouraging and supportive. I didn't think too much about it at the time; I simply enjoyed it.

> Any dating relationship is a potential marriage relationship, and a marriage partner does more to make or break a person than any other relationship this side of heaven.

You know how things turned out: Margaret and I got engaged and then married. The night before our wedding, Dad sat me down and talked to me. Then his and Mom's strong increase in encouragement those years before suddenly made sense. Dad told me that when he saw that Margaret and I were starting to get serious, one day he drove to Chillicothe, the town 12 miles away where Margaret lived. He spent the day meeting with the people who knew Margaret best: her parents, the principal at the high school she attended, and her pastor. He had thought she was the right kind of girl for me, but he wanted to be sure she was a strong Christian of good character before he actively encouraged the relationship.

Because dating relationships are so significant, Margaret and I have established rules for Elizabeth and Joel Porter. Before any boy was allowed to take Elizabeth out on a date, he was required to meet me first. We'd sit and talk. I would ask him questions about his interests, learn a little about his family, and, most importantly, find out if he was a Christian. (If he wasn't, he wasn't allowed to date her.) During our talk, I would also explain our values and expectations.

At first, this process really upset Elizabeth. I remember one day when she was 16. She came to us, asking if she could go out with a boy, and I said, "When will you bring him by so I can meet him?"

Immediately, she burst into tears. "Dad," she cried, "why does he have to meet you? No one's ever going to date me!"

I put my arm around her and gave her a hug. Then I told her, "Honey, our goal is not to keep boys from dating you. We just want to keep the *wrong* people from dating you."

We've also required Joel Porter to bring the girls he wants to date to the house so we can meet them. Once again, we spend time getting to know them, their family background, and their spiritual lives. We also talk to them about our values and expectations for Joel.

"We expect Joel to treat you with courtesy and respect," I tell them. "We expect him to open the car door for you, be kind to you, and act like a gentleman in every way, just as he has seen me do with his mother. If he ever neglects to do that, we want you to let us know right away."

THE PICTURE OF A GOOD MATE

I recently saw the results of a survey on marriage in *Parade* magazine. It showed that people who grew up with happily married parents were more likely to be happily married themselves, and they often married people with similar backgrounds. When children grow up with a positive marriage model in the home, they know what a good mate looks like. But others don't. They're like a little girl I heard about whose teacher asked her students to draw a picture of what they would like to be someday. The little girl was stumped. "I want to be married," she said, "but I don't know how to draw it."

If you talk to a dozen people, you'll get at least a dozen different criteria that they used to choose a mate. Some are like the single woman who prayed, "Father in heaven, hear my prayer, grant it if you can./I've hung a pair of trousers here, please fill them with a man!"

Others often have a stronger sense of what makes a good spouse. Lois Wyse offered these suggestions in *Good Housekeeping* magazine:

1. Watch him drive in heavy traffic.
2. Play tennis with him.
3. Listen to him talk to his mother when he doesn't know you're listening.
4. See how he treats those who serve him (waiters, maids).

5. Notice what he's willing to spend his money to buy.
6. Look at his friends.

    And if you still can't make up your mind, then look at his shoes. A man who keeps his shoes in good repair generally tends to the rest of his life too.[1]

There's wisdom in her words because you can get a glimpse of a person from his or her actions. But I think children need more to go on than those guidelines.

Let me begin to draw for you a picture of a good mate. It's the same picture we've drawn and put before our children over the years. I'll start by giving you the top three qualities Margaret and I value in a mate for our children. Then you finish the picture by adding the qualities you see as important for the partners of your children.

Good Family Background

The picture begins with a good family background. People have long known that family background influences a person's emotional makeup, but studies now show that emotional well-being plays a greater role in success than any other factor, including intelligence.

Here are the qualities we consider to make up a positive family background:

- *Childhood happiness*
- *A positive relationship between parents and child*
- *Home discipline that was firm but not harsh*
- *No family history of physical, alcohol, or substance abuse*
- *A positive attitude*
- *A good self-image and strong sense of security*

It's certainly possible for a person to overcome a poor family background; there are many success stories of people who have done exactly that. In fact, a person who has diligently worked through the difficult issues of a poor background to become healthy is to be admired. But for every person who has gone through that process, there are many more who haven't. You wouldn't want to encourage a child to marry someone who not only hasn't worked though those difficulties but may never intend to do it. Instead, try to give your children the best odds for a good marriage.

Similar Values

People who don't share common values often have a difficult time getting along. Values determine the choices we make, and as a result, they have a lot to do with how we live—moment by moment, day by day, year by year.

In a broad sense, anything a person considers important could be called a value. Here are the ones we've always considered most important in a potential spouse for our children:

1. Christian faith. As a pastor, I've met quite a few engaged couples where one person was a Christian and the other wasn't. Some have come to me to be married, and I've refused to do it. I believe those relationships were headed for trouble. After all, the Bible tells us not to be unequally yoked to unbelievers (see 2 Cor. 6:14).

A while back, I saw a "Dear Abby" column that treated this subject. Someone wrote:

> DEAR ABBY:
> I think you were right when you told that 15-year-old girl to date boys of her own faith. I had parents who tried to tell me that, but I didn't listen. I was raised Catholic, but I fell madly in love with a Lutheran boy. (He converted to marry me.)
> Now 22 years later, I go to church alone, and our four children don't go to church at all. When they were youngsters, they went with me. Their father went occasionally, but his heart wasn't really in it, and he slowly drifted away from the church. Soon the children stopped going too.
> I go to church because it is a vital part of my life. We never know when love will hit, and when it does, it becomes the most important thing in your life. I love my husband, but there is something missing because we don't share our prayers and religious faith. Perhaps I shouldn't complain. It only hurts on Sundays.
> —THINKING OUT LOUD

DEAR THINKING: Yours was a refreshing relief from the many letters stating that dating was a far cry from marrying. However, I still maintain that dating usually leads to marriage. And if religion is an important part of your life, shop only in a store you can buy from.

If that kind of thing happens with two people who grew up in churches, think of what could happen between a believer and a nonbeliever. And if the person of faith is an evangelical Christian whose faith is woven into every aspect of life, it will hurt on more days than just Sunday.

2. Family life. Another area where values need to be similar is family life. When one person in the marriage places a high priority on family and the other doesn't, there's bound to be deep conflict, especially when you consider that the average person spends a high percentage of his lifetime at home. Margaret and I talked about our beliefs concerning family before we were married. We even discussed wanting to adopt children back then. Can you imagine what might have happened if we had gotten married without talking about it and later found that one of us wanted to adopt and the other didn't? It would have caused incredible conflict and pain.

3. Generosity. As I mentioned in breakthrough #4, generosity is important to Margaret and me. When that quality is present in people, it pervades every part of their lives and attitudes. As George Matthew Adams said, "I have never met an unhappy giver." A willingness to give is always a quality of high value, but it's particularly crucial in a marriage. It takes not only commitment for a marriage to work, but also a willingness by each partner to give 100 percent.

> A willingness to give is always a quality of high value, but it's particularly crucial in a marriage.

4. Moral purity. From the time Elizabeth and Joel Porter were little, Margaret and I talked to them about moral purity and its importance to God. We've continued to talk to them about it. They know that sex before marriage is wrong, and we've told them that we waited for our wedding night despite a four-year engagement. Purity is a value we've always cherished and want them to cherish—in spite of the conflicting messages our society sends out.

When Elizabeth was in high school, I gave her a copy of a piece I found in "Dear Abby." It describes well how love and sex before marriage don't mix. It's called "What Is Real Love?"

> Girls need to "prove their love" through illicit sex relations like a moose needs a hat rack. Why not "prove your love" by sticking your head in the oven and turning on the gas? And how about playing leapfrog in the traffic? It's about as safe.
>
> Clear the cobwebs out of your head. Any fellow who asks you to prove your love is trying to take you for the biggest, most gullible fool who ever walked. That "proving" bit is one of the rottenest lines ever invented.
>
> Does he love you? It doesn't sound like it.
>
> Someone who loves you wants whatever is best for you. But now figure it out. He wants you to: Commit an immoral act . . . surrender your virtue . . . throw away your self-respect . . . risk the loss of your precious reputation . . . and risk getting into trouble. Does that sound as though he wants what's best for you? That is the biggest laugh of the century. He wants what's best for him; he wants a thrill he can brag about at your expense. Love? Who's kidding whom?
>
> A guy who loves a girl would sooner cut off his right arm than hurt her. In my opinion, this self-serving so-and-so has proved that he doesn't love you. The predictable aftermath of proof of this kind always finds Don Juan tiring of his sport. That's when he drops you, picks up his line and goes casting elsewhere for bigger and equally foolish fish. If he loves you, let him prove his love—at the altar.

And besides that, moral purity *before* marriage is usually a reliable indicator of ongoing moral purity and faithfulness *after* the wedding.

The Ability to Complement Each Other

The third characteristic that makes up the picture of a good mate is the person's ability to complement his or her marriage partner. We read in Genesis, "The LORD God said, 'It isn't good for the man to live alone. I need to make a suitable partner for him.' . . . That's why a man will leave his own father and mother. He marries a woman, and the two of them become like one person" (2:18, 24, CEV).

Different areas can contribute to a complementary relationship: temperaments, gifts, interests, natural abilities. These factors can both bring out the best in the other person and minimize weaknesses.

Margaret and I, for example, complement each other well. I help her have more fun, and she helps keep me from playing too much. She's practical, and I'm optimistic. She provides a sense of style and an artistic flair to our home and lives. I have highly developed people skills and am good at meeting people and putting them at ease. She has given the children structure and routine, which provide security, and I offer lots of encouragement and unconditional love. Alone, each of us would be out of balance. Together, we're a dynamite team!

Good family background, similar values, and complementary personalities—these are the components of our picture of a good mate. Now you draw the picture of a good spouse to show your children. List the top three to five qualities you will emphasize to your children:

1. _____
2. _____
3. _____
4. _____
5. _____

The marriage partner is certainly the most important influencer our children will have in their lives, though they will be exposed to a lot of influencers along the way. Influencing the influencers in your children's lives is an ongoing process. It begins from the time they're born, and it continues until they leave the nest. Children will resist your desire to influence them at times, but don't give in to their pressure. After they leave home, they'll have their entire lives to make their own choices. Until then, help them to choose wisely by doing all you can to influence their influencers.

Breakthrough #8

Take Your Child Down Memory Lane

The potential breakthrough for the parent . . .
a bridge to the child

The potential breakthrough for the child . . .
bondedness with the family

For more than 15 years, my brother, my sister, and I have lived some distance from one another. So now when all three of us gather together, it's a real occasion. The most recent reunion was just a few weeks ago, when we all flew to Orlando for the wedding of Larry's son, Todd. One night at dinner, the three of us started to reminisce. We talked about our living room wrestling matches, our visits to Grandpa Maxwell's farm at Thanksgiving, and—best of all—the great times we had at the swimming hole.

The swimming hole was a special spot in the creek out back of Moat's farm in Circleville, Ohio. It was at a bend in the creek—wide and deep, with a sandy bank on one side and big trees hanging over the water. Our family discovered the spot, but it soon became the favorite place to swim for all our friends and their families. Over the years, we put up a swinging rope and Dad built us a diving board. That's where I learned to swim; Charles Conrad, my buddy Phil's dad, taught me there one summer.

We spent a lot of hours swimming, battling each other in inner tubes, and trying to outdive each other. And on those really hot summer days, we would go blackberry swimming. Larry and I would hike over to the swimming hole, and each of us would fill up two pails of blackberries really fast. Then we'd swim for a couple of hours. When we were tired, we'd take the blackberries back to Mom, and she would bake a pie. Life didn't get any better than that!

As Larry, Trish, Mom, Dad, and I talked into the late hours that night in Florida, our discussion confirmed in my mind several ideas that I had been thinking about as I worked on this book:

- Our childhood was filled with many pleasant memories.
- The joy we experienced in childhood stemmed from shared activities, not things.
- Our experiences together as children made us feel very close to one another and our parents—both then and now.

I explained these thoughts to the family. When I said that I thought our childhood happiness came from good times together instead of things, Dad chimed in, "That's true, Son. As a parent, don't worry that you can't give children the best of everything. Just give them your best."

Dad's right. All we can do is give our best. Our hope—and I think it's the hope of every Christian parent—is that our children will be close to God and close to the family.

WHAT BONDS FAMILIES TOGETHER

Do you ever wonder why one family seems bonded closely together and another doesn't? There are many theories about what makes people care about one another and want to spend time together. I believe that a home with the following two elements will promote long-lasting bonding among family members:

1. Unconditional love. Deep down, everyone seeks unconditional love, which says, "I love you because you belong to me —nothing more and nothing less."

2. Good memories. Closely bonded families have memories of good times together. Memories are like snapshots—moments in time when positive experiences come together with unconditional love for family members.

HOW TO TAKE YOUR FAMILY DOWN MEMORY LANE

Every parent can create pleasant family memories. It doesn't matter what your background is, where you live, or how much money you make. All it takes is determination and a strategy to make it happen.

If you use the following five factors, you'll provide your children with memories that will bond them to the family.

1. TIME

I heard the story of a state trooper who was riding the highways one day when he saw a large truck with a completely closed aluminum trailer moving erratically in the slow lane. The truck went fast for about a mile. Then it started to slow down until finally it came to a stop on the shoulder. The driver jumped out of the truck, ran back to the trailer, and beat the side of it with a long stick. After about three minutes of frenzied pounding, the driver dashed back to the cab of the truck, climbed in, and immediately sped off down the highway. As the trooper watched, the truck driver repeated the process every mile or two. Finally, the trooper couldn't take it anymore, and he pulled the driver over to find out what was going on.

"Well, officer," the man explained, "this is a one-ton truck, and I'm trying to haul two tons of canaries, so I have to keep half of them in the air at all times!"

Most families today are like that. They're trying frantically to keep too many things up in the air, and the effort is causing their lives to be frenzied. I read a piece by Natasha Tosefowitz that describes the situation:

> I have not seen the plays in town
> only the computer printouts
> I have not read the latest books
> only the *Wall Street Journal*
> I have not heard birds sing this year
> only the ringing of phones
> I have not taken a walk anywhere
> but from the parking lot to my office
> I have not shared a feeling in years
> but my thoughts are known to all
> I have not listened to my own needs
> but what I want I get
> I have not shed a tear in ages
> I have arrived.
> Is this where I was going?[1]

In July 1995, I resigned my position as senior pastor of Skyline Wesleyan Church in San Diego. One reason was that I just didn't have enough time with my family—not the kind of time I wanted to give. Time is quickly becoming our most precious commodity, and overcommitment is its enemy. If we don't give our families enough time, our relationships suffer. Children spell *love* T-I-M-E. We can try to kid ourselves about giving them quality time, but if there's no *quantity* of time, there can be no *quality* time.

I read a statistic that compared the amount of time parents spend with their children today versus the amount of time they spent in the past. A century ago, parents spent an average of 54 percent of their waking hours with their children. The current average is 18 percent—one-third of the time spent before. No wonder families are becoming increasingly fragmented!

How to Establish Time Priorities

To avoid having regrets tomorrow, learn to establish time priorities today. Only when you actively, purposely *plan and take time* for your family will you find that you actually *have time* for your family.

Here are some tips Margaret and I have used to carve out time for each other and the kids. I believe they will help you, too:

Schedule family time first. About 10 years ago, my speaking and teaching calendar really started getting full. Margaret and I decided the only way to guarantee family time was to schedule it in advance. From then on, we put important family dates on the calendar first: birthdays, graduations, the kids' ball games, recitals, and so on. And we wrote in our vacations a year ahead. Then, when I set my work agenda each month, I planned around the family events. I often

> The only way to guarantee family time is to schedule it in advance.

had to work late several days or to work on the weekends to be able to keep a family date open. It hasn't always been easy, but it has remained a priority.

Discuss plans with the children. When children are little, we get in the habit of expecting them to live their lives on our schedule. But as they get older and begin to be more independent, we can no longer do that—not if we want to continue having good family time with them.

Margaret and I let the children know in advance when we have something planned for the family. We give them as much notice as we can, and we ask them to write it on their calendars. This provides two benefits: It makes them a part of the planning process, and it gets them to also schedule family time first. Any time a parent springs a family event on teenagers at the last minute, he's asking for conflict.

Put your family agenda ahead of your personal agenda. As I've planned my calendar, I've always scheduled family first, work next, then personal activities. I guess that's why I've had so few days for leisure activities over the years. The negative result has been that I haven't taken care of myself as I'd like to have done. For example, I haven't gotten enough exercise. But it's been a trade-off I've been willing to make. I didn't ever want to look back at the time my kids were growing up and regret not spending time with them. Now I'm trying to get better about setting aside time for myself, but I'll always put my family's agenda ahead of my own.

When possible, change your work schedule to attend significant events. When Elizabeth was about nine years old, she was given the chance to sing her first solo ever. It was going to be in a production at school. I was heartbroken because it looked as if I wouldn't be able to see her do it. I was scheduled to teach a leadership conference in Indianapolis—an event that had been planned a year in advance. The conference was to run all day Tuesday and Wednesday and a half day on Thursday. Elizabeth's production was on Thursday evening, but my plane wouldn't arrive in San Diego until after her solo was over.

On Wednesday night, after I finished the second day of the conference, I sat in my hotel room thinking about Elizabeth and her solo. I kept wondering, *How can I get back in time to see her?* Then I had an idea. I called my secretary back in San Diego and asked her to change my plane tickets to an earlier flight. Then I called Margaret and told her I would be home in time, but not to tell Elizabeth.

The next morning, I started the conference right on time, and I talked to the attending pastors about Elizabeth, her solo, and my dilemma. Then I told them, "I've figured out a way to see Elizabeth this evening if you will permit me to do it. If we get started right away, I teach you quickly, and we agree not to take any breaks, I'll be able to catch an earlier flight. I promise I'll teach you everything I originally intended to, but I just won't take as long.

"Will you allow me to do that so I can see my daughter sing her very first solo tonight?"

The group went wild, cheering and clapping. And when it was time to finish the conference that morning and I thanked them for allowing me to go early, they stood and cheered as I left.

I made it to the plane and back to San Diego on time. I'll never forget the expression on Elizabeth's face when she realized I would be home for her solo. She wrote me a touching thank-you note and gave it to me the next day. I've always cherished that note and the memory of her singing.

You may not travel in your business and may never have a situation similar to the one I faced with Elizabeth, but there will probably be times when your children will be part of an event that's significant to them and you'll be scheduled to work. I encourage you to find a way to get time off for those events. If you're a manager, schedule yourself off during your child's recital, ball game, graduation, or whatever. If your work schedule varies, such as it does for a firefighter or restaurant server, trade schedules with a colleague. Or if you can take half a day's vacation or a long lunch hour, do that. Some events come only once in your child's life, and if you miss them, they're gone forever. Try your best to share major events with your children. It will make a lasting impression on them and build a bond that lasts.

2. TALKING

Dr. John Baucom said, "With the appearance of the two-bathroom home, Americans forgot how to cooperate. With the appearance of the two-car family, we forgot how to associate, and with the coming of the two-television home, we forgot how to communicate."

Poor or nonexistent communication is the greatest problem many parents face with their children. No matter what the cause, parents and children are talking to one another less each day. Twenty years ago, I saw the results of a survey conducted by family-life specialists Delmer W. Holbrook and his wife. It reported the three things fathers say most often when responding to their kids:

1. "I'm too tired."
2. "We don't have enough money."
3. "Keep quiet."[2]

As bad as those results were, I think conditions were better 20 years ago than they are today. I'd hate to see what results their survey would get now.

One of the best ways to promote communication is to catch your children when *they* want to talk. Margaret and I have tried to do this by making ourselves available at certain times every day. For example, Margaret has always tried to be home when the kids arrive from school. We've eaten dinner together as a family as often as possible. I've taken the kids to school in the mornings and left the radio off so we could talk. And we've had regular prayer times with each child every day.

The keys to communicating with children are *availability* and *perseverance*. You have to make yourself available to children at times when they may want to talk. Prime times are right before bedtime, first thing in the morning, and right after school. So are times when you're out having fun with your kids—if they feel safe and loved, they're more likely to share things with you. And when they become less communicative, don't give up. Continue to love them and listen.

3. TRADITIONS

I love traditions. Besides being fun, they preserve a family's heritage and give each family member a sense of shared identity. Things of value can be handed down from generation to generation through traditions. And once a practice has been established within the family, you'll find that children look forward to it as a vital part of an event.

When most people hear the word *tradition,* they think of things that happen once each year. But annual traditions aren't the only type worth observing. Consider the following possibilities:

Milestone Traditions

Some events come along only once in a lifetime for each child—the first day of school, the sixteenth birthday, making the varsity team, high-school graduation, the day the child receives Christ, and so on. Any day that marks a milestone can be made special by a celebration. And that can become a family tradition.

But beware: If you have more than one child and you celebrate a milestone with the first one, you can be sure the others will expect you to do it with them. Even if you don't intend to make it a tradition, they'll want you to.

Annual Traditions

Just because annual traditions are the most common doesn't mean they aren't great ideas. Children eagerly look forward to traditions, not only because they're fun, but also because they give a sense of continuity. One of my favorite traditions when I was little was our annual trip to Grandpa Maxwell's house for Thanksgiving. Every year when Dad pulled the car into my grandparents' driveway, he'd honk the horn, and Grandma and Grandpa would wave from the kitchen window and then come to the door to greet us. And many of the things we'd do were the same each year: Grandpa always wrestled me and Larry in his living room (now you know where Dad got the idea); we always ate turkey, sweet potatoes, and applesauce for dinner; Grandpa always took each of us kids aside and prayed for us; and we always went to the field to visit his cows—who came when you called them by name.

Our kids have missed out on some holiday traditions because we've lived so far from the rest of the family. But Margaret and I have tried to add some traditions of our own to make up for it. For example, every summer, we take a trip to Lawrence Welk Village, a resort north of San Diego. We spend a whole week there; the kids ride their bikes, rollerblade, fish, play tennis, and meet new friends. It's a fun, relaxing family time to which we all look forward.

You may already have meaningful annual traditions in your family—for birthdays, Thanksgiving, Christmas, or the Fourth of July. If you do, that's great. But if your family members are scattered across the country, that doesn't mean you can't have traditions, too. Plan events for just your immediate family members. Or do things with friends or neighbors. Create your own traditions, just as we have.

Weekly Traditions

Annual and milestone traditions build long-term bonds, but weekly traditions can sometimes build an immediate bridge between parents and children. We've just developed a new one for Friday nights. As I mentioned earlier, not long ago, my sister, Trish, her husband, Steve, and their kids moved to San Diego. We've really enjoyed their company, especially after not having any family close for more than a decade. Now on Friday of each week, we go over to their house to have hamburgers and watch a movie. All of us— parents and kids—look forward to the get-together.

Daily Traditions

Daily events make children feel secure and lend a sense of continuity in the home. Eating dinner together, having devotions each morning, and praying with children at bedtime are notable examples of daily traditions.

It takes discipline on the part of the parent to maintain daily traditions, especially when life gets busy. And children may complain about them. But as they grow up, they appreciate them and often think back to them with fondness.

A Legacy of Traditions

Margaret has always had a sense of family history. From the time the children were little, she has kept a record of them in their baby books. She's written in important information about their development: when they got their first teeth, when they walked, when they accepted Christ. The children's whole history is there, complete with photographs. When the children get married and start their own homes, she'll give them their baby books.

Margaret has also started other traditions for them. Let me tell you about her latest. Think back to last Christmas. As you were out shopping, you probably saw lots of ceramic houses and buildings for Christmas villages. For a number of years, Margaret has been buying several of those each Christmas. I'm guessing we have between 25 and 30 of them. But they're not all for us. She's getting them for Elizabeth and Joel. Someday, when they've got their own families, they'll get the village pieces that have been picked out for them, and they'll have a bit of their own childhood Christmas right under their trees.

Your kids would probably love that kind of thing, too. Think about some traditions you can start with them for the future. Give them a legacy to pass along to their children.

4. TRIPS

By now, you probably realize trips are significant to the Maxwell family. Margaret and I decided early in our marriage that she should be included in exciting trips I was to take. I was to be her companion in life, not a storyteller. As a result, we've taken wonderful trips together—as a couple and as a family.

When I was growing up, we took quite a few family trips. And no matter where we were going or how far we were traveling, Dad always stopped driving at 3:00 and picked out a motel with a swimming pool so we could play in the water before dinner.

The Trip Down the Street May Change Your Life

Not all our trips were of the vacation variety. Occasionally, Dad took us on other trips that also had a profound impact and gave us memories of a different kind.

I remember Dad driving Larry and me to Hillsborough, Ohio, one Saturday morning. He said we were going to visit some children in a home. We weren't exactly sure what he meant, but I was happy to go. I always loved meeting and playing with new kids.

When we drove up to a big, institutional, brick building, I realized that my idea of a home didn't match where we had arrived. We checked in with the people at the front desk, and from the way Dad talked, it sounded as though he had been there before. One of the nurses offered to take us on a tour, so we followed her from room to room.

The place was filled with kids of all ages and sizes. But I could see right away that every one of them had some kind of problem. Some kids were missing arms or legs. Others were mentally disabled. Their speech was slurred and babyish, even though they were older than me. I tried hard not to stare.

Dad talked comfortably with the kids, and he asked Larry and me to visit and play with them. Larry and I shot marbles with a kid who had only a thumb and one index finger on each hand. Once we stopped staring at the places where his other fingers should have been, we started treating him like a regular kid, especially since he was beating us. On the way home, Dad talked to us about how fortunate we were and about the wonderful blessings God had showered on us. And deep in our hearts, we agreed with him.

Another time, when I was 11 or 12, Dad took me to Lowery Lane in Circleville. It was the poorest section of town. We drove there in the snow, and Dad had us get out of the car and walk around. The houses were small and old. I saw one house where the window had been broken and it had been replaced with a piece of cardboard—not much help against the fierce wind. People moved from place to place in shabby clothes. I still remember one man who walked past us who had on nothing heavier than a suit jacket, even though it must have been about 20 degrees. He had the lapel turned up in an attempt to keep out the cold.

That trip to Lowery Lane stayed with me for years. It touched my heart in a way that 100 eloquent sermons couldn't. Years later, when I was a student at Circleville Bible College, I used to go down to Lowery Lane to preach with a couple of friends, hoping Jesus would touch lives in a way the world hadn't.

The Trip That Made the Difference

When Trish was in junior high school, Dad took her on a special trip that affected the rest of her life. A couple of years before, she had decided she wanted to become a nurse. So when Dad went to visit Nancy Graham, a friend who was in the hospital dying of leukemia, he took Trish along.

Dad was a little concerned about how Trish would react. By that time, Nancy was in pretty bad shape. She had lost a lot of weight and was haggard and gray. But when they got to her room and Dad introduced Trish, my sister went right over to the sick woman, held her hand, and talked to her as if she had been caring for people all her life. Dad could see she had compassion for her, and at that moment he knew Trish had truly been called to the medical field. He and Mom gave her nothing but encouragement to pursue her dream after that.

Maybe you've never considered taking your children on shorter trips, the kind you can take without ever leaving your town. If you haven't, watch your children to see what kinds of trips would benefit them. And start looking around for opportunities. The trip down the street may turn out to make the difference in your children's lives.

5. TENDERNESS

We walk down memory lane so we can bond with our children. Of all human experiences, tenderness is the best vehicle for bonding. Tenderness involves loving, encouraging touch and emotional commitment.

Physical Tenderness (Touch)

Touch has the incredible ability to heal people and bond them to one another. We've all heard stories about what happens to newborn children when they're deprived of physical touch and affection. Many become withdrawn and die.

| Touch has the incredible ability to heal people and bond them to one another. | Not only do we have modern studies that promote the benefits of positive touch, but we also have the New Testament, which gives |

us plenty of examples of the power of touch. Jesus touched people when He healed them (see Matt. 8:3). He washed His disciples' feet (see John 13:5). The disciples laid their hands on people when they prayed for them (see Acts 6:6). And early Christians made it a habit to embrace (see Acts 20:36-38). Paul even encouraged them to greet each other with a holy kiss (see Rom. 16:16).

I was fortunate to have grown up in an expressive family. My parents hugged and kissed a lot, and they were affectionate with us kids as well. They'd hug us, kiss us, and put their arms around our shoulders or sit close to us when they spoke words of love and encouragement. Even to this day, we all hug when we greet one another.

Margaret and I are affectionate and have had the same kind of relationship with Elizabeth and Joel Porter. It's been easy for us because of our upbringing. But maybe that hasn't been the case for you. If it hasn't, I encourage you to change. Break the cycle, and make your family one of tenderness and affection, a place where your kids see your love for them and your spouse demonstrated every day.

Emotional Tenderness

Emotional tenderness should go hand in hand with physical tenderness. It takes place when family members are sensitive to the needs of one another and commit to meeting those needs appropriately every day.

When author and management expert Stephen Covey discussed healthy interdependent relationships in his book *The Seven Habits of Highly Effective People*, he was describing emotional tenderness. He explained a marriage relationship in terms of an emotional bank account. In a financial bank account, a person makes deposits and builds up a reserve from which to make periodic withdrawals. In an emotional bank account, we make relational deposits that build up trust. Covey noted six major ways a person makes deposits in an emotional bank account. They're good guidelines not only for a marriage, but also for a parent-child relationship:

1. Understanding the individual. Deep down, everyone wants to be understood. Children are no different. As they get older, that desire continues to grow.

2. Attending to the little things. Taking care of the little things communicates tenderness wonderfully. You can do a variety of things that build the relationship—for example, attending to a child's scraped knee, making your child's bed for her as a surprise, cooking his favorite food for dinner, or having the car washed and waxed for your teenager's special date.

3. Keeping commitments. Few things erode trust faster than unkept commitments. Keep your promises. Don't tell the kids you'll take them to Disney World if there's a chance you won't be able to follow through. And be there for your children's recitals, as you said you would. Follow through on the little things, too. If you say you'll take the kids to the park on Saturday, write it down in your calendar and do it—just as you would if it were a business appointment.

4. Clarifying expectations. Have you ever gotten angry with your kids for not doing what you asked, then realized you didn't explain your expectations well enough? If you have, you're eroding their trust in you. A careful and loving explanation on the front end will show your children tenderness and respect. It also sets them up to succeed.

5. Showing personal integrity. Consistency is important to children. When your words and actions match, you're showing them you live a life of integrity, and they're able to trust you.

6. Apologizing sincerely when you make a withdrawal. Finally, when you make mistakes, admit them. When you don't, it drives a wedge between you and your children. They know when they've been wronged. When you don't apologize, it only drives them away from you.[3]

Tenderness brings family members together in a remarkable way. For example, not long ago, I went to Atlanta to teach a two-day leadership conference. I finished the conference at about 4:30 in the afternoon, and I dashed to the airport so I could fly back and spend the night in San Diego. Those return flights from the East Coast can be pretty grueling; it's usually about an eight-hour trip after a 10-hour day of work. And on top of that, I usually try to get some work done on the plane.

That night, my flight got into San Diego at about 11:00, and Margaret picked me up at the airport as she usually does. We talked in the car on the way back to the house, and when we got home, I was ready to go straight up to bed. I was totally worn out—and I'm not a night person anyway.

I dropped my bag to the floor as I entered our bedroom, kicked off my shoes, and began to get undressed. And then I heard a voice from down the hall: "Dad, I'm still awake!"

It was Joel. It was almost midnight (a couple of hours past his bedtime), and though he had gone to bed, he had stayed awake—as he often does when I get home from a trip. He wanted me to come to his room, rub his back, and pray for him as I do every night when I'm home.

"I'm coming, Honey," I called to him. Even as tired as I was, I walked down the hall and spent 20 minutes talking to him about his week, telling him about my trip, rubbing his back, and praying with him. It was a tender time. It's something Joel looks forward to, even at age 17. And it's something I also look forward to. I want to enjoy it while I can. It won't be long before Joel is grown up and moves away.

Even after that happens, however, there will always be a bond between us, a bond built not only on the relationship we've maintained, but also on the memories we share.

Breakthrough #9

Don't Wait for the Church to Grow Your Child Spiritually

The potential breakthrough for the parent . . .
the creation of a spiritual legacy

The potential breakthrough for the child . . .
the creation of a spiritual foundation

When I was 13 years old, my parents sent me to Christian summer camp. That wasn't unusual; I went just about every year. In fact, I was well known at camp because I was such a cutup. I remember that one year when I arrived, a couple of counselors grabbed me, took me aside, and searched my suitcase for contraband—like balloons for staging water balloon fights, peanut butter for putting in people's shoes, shaving cream for lathering sleeping campers' faces, and other things like that. They were smugly gratified when they discovered I hadn't brought anything like that in my suitcase that year. I was also pleased—I had suspected they would search me, and I'd given all those kinds of things to my friends to sneak in for me.

I was really looking forward to camp again. The day I was getting ready to leave, Dad said he wanted to have a talk with me. He sat me down on my bed and said, "John, this is going to be a special year for you at camp. I believe God is going to speak to you, and I'm praying that when He does, you will obey Him." Then he put his arm around me and said, "God has something big planned for you, Son, something special."

Dad was right about camp. God did speak to me, and during a worship time in the camp's meeting hall, I went forward and rededicated my life to Christ. It was an important step in my spiritual journey.

A PARENT'S FIRST AND MOST FUNDAMENTAL RESPONSIBILITY

Camp was only one of the many positive spiritual influences in my growing-up years. My father and mother took an active hand in their kids' spiritual development. They knew their first and most fundamental responsibility was to teach us to put God first. After all, as parents, they were the ones who got the first and most influential shot at it.

Over the years, I've met many parents who expect the church to develop their children spiritually. Though the church does take part in the process, it's unrealistic for parents to hope their children will receive a firm spiritual foundation from people who spend only an hour or two with their kids once a week.

My father learned this lesson as a young man from Dr. John R. Church. Dad heard the preacher speak once on "Three Things We Can't Expect the Church to Instill in Our Children: Religion, Discipline, and Honesty." Dad told me that Dr. Church's message left a strong impression on him, and from that time forward, he took it as his and Mom's responsibility to train us kids spiritually.

LEARNING FROM THE PATRIARCHS

Deuteronomy 6:6-9 states, "These commandments that I give you today are to be upon your hearts. *Impress them on your children.* Talk about them when you sit at home and when you walk along the road, when you lie down and when you get up. Tie them as symbols on your hands and bind them on your foreheads. Write them on the doorframes of your houses and on your gates" (emphasis added). It's clear from this passage that parents have the responsibility of giving children spiritual instruction, and that instruction should be a continual way of life, not a periodic lesson.

Moses, the writer of Deuteronomy, understood the value of parental teaching. He would not have been the man he became if it hadn't been for his mother. You may remember the story: Moses was born into slavery in Egypt at a time when Pharaoh ordered that all male Hebrew babies be put to death.

But Moses' mother, Jochebed, put him in a basket in the Nile, and he was rescued by Pharaoh's daughter. The princess decided Moses would live, and he was given to a Hebrew woman to be nursed. That woman was his own mother, Jochebed.

She had him only a few years. But during that time, she must have taught him to love and serve God, because despite a privileged upbringing in Pharaoh's palace and an Egyptian education, he still identified with the Hebrew people and their God. When it was time for Moses to choose between going the way of the world or serving God, he chose to serve God. It's the same choice each of our children has to face.

SEVEN GOALS FOR PUTTING GOD FIRST

What does it mean to develop children spiritually? Ask 10 people and you'll probably get 10 different answers. One person will tell you it depends on extensive Scripture memorization. Another will say it means praying for an hour every day. Still another might say you should be sure your children make a commitment to Christ and then let the church do the rest.

I believe spiritual maturity comes from a variety of things. Years ago, Margaret and I identified seven goals for our children that we thought would develop them spiritually. Our desire is that they . . .

1. *Love Jesus as Lord and Savior, having a personal relationship with Him.*
2. *Understand the importance and meaning of prayer, and recognize God's answers.*
3. *Read the Bible, and apply it to their lives.*
4. *Live holy, obedient lives marked by love and service to others.*
5. *Become active members of a local church, and use their gifts and talents to support it.*
6. *Worship and praise God as a routine of life.*
7. *Tell others about their relationship with Christ.*

Our plan was to encourage our children in those seven areas. We determined that if we could help achieve each of them, we would have done all we could to lead them toward spiritual maturity.

Most parents would agree that our seven goals are worthwhile, but the way to achieve them would be more difficult to agree upon. I find that some parents get mixed up when it comes to where their responsibilities end and their children's begin. They want to make the spiritual choices *for* their children, and sometimes they don't focus enough attention on their own choices.

The best we can do is to show our children what's right, teach them how to learn and apply spiritual truths, and ask God to help them make the right choices. That's why Margaret and I have focused on three areas when it comes to developing our children spiritually: modeling, application, and prayer.

MODELING: WHAT ONLY PARENTS CAN DO

Modeling is at the heart of helping children develop spiritually. You must first go in the direction you would have your children go. As Albert Schweitzer said, "Example is not the main thing in influencing others . . . it is the only thing." I understood this in a big way after a conversation I had with my dad when I was in my early twenties. I had already accepted the call to preach, and I was attending Circleville Bible College. I was also in the last year of my long engagement to Margaret. She and I were extremely attracted to each other, and every time we went on a date, we were fighting the temptation to go further than we should in our physical relationship. One night, I approached

> As Albert Schweitzer said, "Example is not the main thing in influencing others ... it is the only thing."

my dad, because I wanted to talk to him about it and get his advice.

"Let's go sit outside and talk about it," he said.

We went out and sat on the porch together. I told him that Margaret and I were still morally pure, but that we were struggling. Each day was getting harder and harder.

"You know, John," he said, "what you're facing is something every young man faces. I faced it myself. But let me tell you something." He looked straight at me—eye to eye. "I've always been faithful to your mother. And I kept myself pure before she and I got married. Let me tell you why. It's not that I haven't been tempted or had opportunities.

"John, I've observed in the Bible that when the father is unfaithful, his son is often unfaithful," Dad said. "The first generation that sins opens the door for the next generation to do the same thing. Jacob was deceptive to his father when he pretended to be Esau, and later he was deceived by his sons concerning Joseph. David committed adultery with Bathsheba, and Solomon had problems with women that drew him away from God.

"Son, I've remained pure not only for your mother, myself, and God, but also for you, Larry, and Trish. My father was faithful. I've remained faithful. And I pray you will be faithful not only for yourself and your bride, but also for *your* children."

After that, Dad helped me set up some guidelines to help us remain pure, such as Margaret's and my agreement that one of us would leave if things got too steamy. We had a lot of 15-minute dates the rest of that year!

That night, Dad also agreed to help keep me accountable. His example really made an impression on me—enough to help me refrain from sex until Margaret's and my wedding night.

Wear Shoes You Want Filled

I once preached a sermon called "Wear Shoes You Want Filled." The thesis was that the example we set does a lot to determine how our children will turn out. The sermon looked at the Old Testament example of Lot, the nephew of Abraham, who lived in the sinful city of Sodom. Lot made some critical mistakes that hurt not only him, but also destroyed his family (see Gen. 13; 19).

Lot's life had the wrong . . .

- *Emphasis.* He placed financial prosperity over spiritual health.
- *Environment.* He expected his family to live in Sodom and not be like the Sodomites.
- *Expectation.* He thought he could change Sodom's negative society by

becoming a part of it.

- *Example.* He believed his family's actions would reflect his words instead of his lifestyle.
- *Entanglements.* He didn't know how much the world had influenced him and his family until it was too late.

As parents, if we believe that we can live according to the world's rules and still expect our children to follow God's rules, we're only fooling ourselves, and we'll eventually find ourselves in a position of failure, just as Lot did.

The Modeling Your Children Deserve

Choosing God and embracing His values instead of the world's are only the beginning when it comes to setting a good example. It takes living a moral life and having a desire to be strategic. Here are 10 guidelines to help you be a good model to your children.

Your children deserve . . .

1. To hear you pray earnestly and often. Children learn about prayer and our relationship with God based on the example we set for them in prayer. If they see us praying only at meals, or if our prayers aren't heartfelt, they'll get a limited picture of who God is.

Pray all the time (see 1 Thess. 5:17). Pray in the morning when you get up. Pray at meals. Pray when you put the children to bed. Pray when you receive bad news and when you receive good news. Pray when you're worried or sick, and when you're celebrating as well. Let your children see and hear how you pray to God your Father all the time.

2. To spend time with you as you talk about the things of God. Many kids think God is someone who lives at church. They put Him in a box because they don't hear much about Him except on Sundays. Help your children understand that God desires to be a part of every aspect of our lives (remember Deut. 6:6-9).

Share God with your children. Talk about Him all the time. Make Him a regular part of your conversation, just like anything else that's important to you.

3. To hear you talk to others about becoming Christians. Jesus has called all Christians to tell others about their faith (see Matt. 28:18-20), but relatively few do. Rebecca Pippert has observed, "Christians and non-Christians have something in common; we're both uptight about evangelism."

If you share your faith often, your children will be more likely to share theirs. It will seem normal to them, and they'll be more likely to follow in your footsteps and become mature, well-rounded Christians.

4. To see you put God first in your giving. Giving is really a spiritual issue, not a financial one, as most people think. God asks us to put Him first, not only in the Ten Commandments, but also elsewhere in Scripture. One example is in Malachi 3:8-10:

> "Will a man rob God? Yet you rob me.
> "But you ask, 'How do we rob you?'
> "In tithes and offerings. You are under a curse—the whole nation of you—because you are robbing me. Bring the whole tithe into the storehouse, that there may be food in my house. Test me in this," says the LORD Almighty, "and see if I will not throw open the floodgates of heaven and pour out so much blessing that you will not have room enough for it."

Wow—what an incredible promise!

As a pastor, I saw a lot of people struggle with this issue. If you haven't yet settled it yourself, I encourage you to do it now. If you wait until you *feel comfortable* putting God first financially, you'll probably never do it. But once you settle the lordship issue by putting God first in your giving, your financial situation will improve. Then you'll also be in a position to teach your children to put God first. If you teach them to give while they're young, they will be blessed and will likely continue putting God first financially all their lives.

5. To watch you live a consistent Christian life. The key to constructive modeling is being a consistent example (see Deut. 10:12-13). Inconsistency confuses children, and because of their sin nature, they're more likely to follow the negative examples than the positive ones. Live the Christian life—there's no better teacher for your children than your Christ-honoring example.

6. To go with you to visit the unfortunate. Visits to people who are sick, poor, shut in, or hurting in some way help children discover their gifts of compassion. Such trips also develop in them appreciation for how God has blessed them. Besides, we're called to minister to those less fortunate than us (see James 1:27).

The next time you visit your sick uncle or go to your grandmother's house to help her with household chores, take your children with you. Your actions will speak louder than any lesson you could teach.

7. To hear you say good things about other Christians. As I said before, growing up, I thought all Christians were perfect, because I never heard my parents say anything negative about other believers. They followed the directive in Scripture that we build up one another (see 1 Thess. 5:11).

Discuss whatever you want with your spouse, but around your children, don't talk about the negative things you see in other Christians. Instead, look for something positive to say. Build the Body of Christ; don't tear it down.

8. To be exposed to experiences that will bring Christian growth. It was never God's intention that we accept His Son as Savior and then never grow beyond that decision. We are to be Christ's disciples (see 1 Tim. 4:13-16), and so are our children.

Teach your children Scripture. Sing hymns and choruses together. Have daily devotions with them. They don't have to be complicated or long. Both our kids received Christ in the car while Margaret was talking with them.

Take your kids to Sunday school and church. Invite them to attend Christian concerts and theater with you. Take them to hear inspiring preachers. Expose them to a variety of growing experiences. And most important, help them to apply what they learn.

9. To see you love your spouse. Treating your spouse with love and respect is not only biblical (see Eph. 5:22-33), but it also teaches children about relationships—not only among family members and friends, but also between them and God. No other relationship does more to help or harm the way children interact with others. Theodore M. Hesburgh had it right when he said, "The most important thing a father can do for his children is to love their mother."

10. To know your Savior in a personal way. Obviously, the goal of all parents should be for their children to know Christ as Savior. That relationship guides and guards them not only during their lifetimes, but for eternity (see John 17:3). Don't wait for an "expert" such as your pastor to present the gospel to your children. Talk to them about it from the time they're born, and one day they may ask you to lead them in a salvation prayer.

APPLICATION: WHAT ONLY CHILDREN CAN DO

A rabbi and a soap maker went for a walk together. The cynical soap maker said, "What good is religion? Look at all the trouble and misery of the world! Still there, even after years—thousands of years—of teaching about goodness and truth and peace. Still there after all the prayers and sermons and teachings. If religion is good and true, why should this be?"

The rabbi said nothing. They continued walking until he noticed a child playing in the gutter. Then the rabbi said, "Look at that child. You say that soap makes people clean, but see the dirt on that youngster? What good is soap? With all the soap in the world, over all these years, that child is still filthy. I wonder how effective soap is, after all!"

"But Rabbi," the soap maker protested, "soap cannot do any good unless it is used!"

"Exactly," replied the rabbi. "Exactly!"

That's a good lesson for us to learn, too. The spiritual truths and disciplines our children learn from us benefit them only as long as they're applied. The good news is that if you model them well, your children will have already seen them in action. But you can't expect children to automatically apply what they've learned without assistance from you—at least not at first. It takes time for them to do that. Your desire, however, should be to help them recognize spiritual truths and become so used to applying what they learn that it becomes a part of their lifestyle.

A good way to help children do that is to take them through the next step after understanding, which is *processing* the information. We try to do that with our kids in a variety of ways. When we've asked them to write a one-page report after listening to an informative cassette tape, it has helped them process the information in the tape. During devotions, we often ask them to interpret a verse and tell how it could be applied to their lives; that also helps them to process information.

I also like to ask the kids questions that will make them think about something they've heard, such as a sermon. I want them to examine themselves in its light.

Here are examples of questions that work well. You can use them or something similar with your children:

- *What was the thesis of the message?* Every message—whether verbal or written—has a thesis, a main idea or truth that it's trying to communicate. Sometimes a thesis is clearly stated in the message and is easy to understand. Other times it's only implied, so it takes some thought to figure out what it is. But every sermon, lesson, article, and book has a central thesis. When people can determine what that is, they can more easily understand the whole message and how to apply it to their lives.

- *Why do you think the author wants to tell people this message?* This question gets children to start the application process without feeling threatened by the message, because it doesn't yet directly involve them.

- *How could this message benefit someone who needs it?* This question helps kids discover some motivation for applying the message.

- *What could you take from the message and apply to your life?* Once children have already identified the main idea and thought about some positive benefits for applying it, this query encourages them to apply the message to themselves in a personal way.

- *How will you apply the message to your life?* To answer, children need to devise a specific plan, which allows for accountability in the future.

Another way to help children apply what they learn is through projects and activities. Singing in the choir, working in productions, going on mission trips, acting as a big brother or sister to a younger child at church—nearly anything that encourages a child to act on a Christian principle he or she has learned can be a reinforcement and application activity.

Most Christians are educated way beyond their level of obedience; that's why they need to be encouraged to apply what they know. It's a truth that has been prevalent in the church for a long time. Even author Mark Twain recognized it nearly a century ago. It's said that a hypocritical Christian once told Twain, "Before I die, I intend to make a pilgrimage to the Holy Land, climb to the very top of Mount Sinai, and read the Ten Commandments out loud."

"I've got a better idea," Twain replied. "Why don't you just stay right where you are and keep them!"

PRAYER: ASKING GOD TO DO WHAT ONLY HE CAN DO

Prayer is the final step in the process of developing our children spiritually. I still remember the first time I overheard my mother praying alone. It was on a Saturday when I was about five or six years old. I had been playing football outside with Larry and his friends—and getting run over a lot. I came in for a glass of water, and as I was chugging it down, I thought I heard my mother talking to someone. It was the middle of the day, and I knew Dad wasn't home, so it couldn't be him. I thought maybe she was on the phone, so I refilled my glass, took it with me, and crept down the hall to right outside the door to her room. It didn't take me but a second to figure out she was praying:

". . . and watch over Melvin and keep him safe as he travels in Ohio today," she said. "I pray that he makes it home safely to his family tonight." I'd heard Mom pray this kind of thing before. I was about to tiptoe back down to the kitchen when all of a sudden, I heard my name.

"Father," she said, "I want to pray a special blessing of protection on Johnny. I love him so much. He is a special child, and I know You have Your hand on him. Lord, I pray that he would always know Your will for his life. And I pray that he would grow up to be a great man of God."

I thought, *Wow! My mother is putting in a good word for me with God Himself!*

"I know Johnny's being tempted a lot to be disobedient right now," she continued. "I pray that You would keep him from that temptation. I know sometimes at school the wrong thing looks mighty good to him, but I pray You'd keep him away from it. When he's tempted to cheat on a test or misbehave, I pray that You would cover him with Your Spirit."

I felt a little surprised that Mom knew about me at school. But I also felt warm and safe when I heard her words. Before, I only heard her prayers said in front of me. I guess I thought that when she prayed over me, she was doing it to make me feel better. I didn't know she prayed for me on her own and because she really wanted to. I slipped back down the hall to the kitchen and went outside, but that wasn't the last time I heard Mom pray like that. Sometimes I'd sit outside her door, unknown to her, and I'd listen to her pray for me, Dad, Larry, Trish, and a host of other people.

Spending time alone on her knees was the most important thing Mom could do for us kids. She communicated with God, asking Him for what *only He* could provide: divine protection and guidance. She put us in God's hands every day.

> **Whether your children are 5 days or 50 years old, prayer is a powerful tool for helping them.**

Prayer is for all time. The teaching you give your children may not affect them strongly after they reach adolescence, and your modeling may have little impact after they leave high school, but whether your children are 5 days or 50 years old, prayer is a powerful tool for helping them.

I'm beginning to understand that concept now more than ever—since Elizabeth is 19 and living away from home. A while back, I found a poem that expresses the idea well:

Dear Children

I can no longer grasp your tiny hand and lead you across the street,
Nor tuck you in at night against the chill,
Nor kiss your precious flawless baby face,
But, I can pray.

I can no longer take you to the House of God,
Nor read to you from His precious Holy Word,
Nor tell you what is right, and what is wrong,
But, I can pray.

For you are grown and from my constant care are gone,
To choose YOUR way and live YOUR life,
And be what you WILL in YOUR own way,
But, I STILL pray.

How to Pray for Your Children

You may already pray for your children, but you may not have a strategy for *how* to pray for them. Below are 12 areas for you to pray about. They're accompanied by Scripture references. Pray the Scriptures over your children regularly for additional blessings from God.

1. *Pray that they will know Christ as Savior early in life* (Ps. 63:1; 2 Tim. 3:15).
2. *Pray that they will have a hatred for sin* (Ps. 97:10).
3. *Pray that they will be caught when guilty* (Ps. 119:71).
4. *Pray that they will be protected from the evil one in each area of their lives: spiritual, emotional, and physical* (John 17:15).
5. *Pray that they will have a responsible attitude in all their interpersonal relationships* (Dan. 6:3).
6. *Pray that they will respect people in authority over them* (Rom. 13:1).
7. *Pray that they will desire the right kind of friends and be protected from the wrong friends* (Prov. 1:10-15).
8. *Pray that they, as well as their mates, will be kept pure* (1 Cor. 6:14-20).
9. *Pray that they will be kept from the wrong mate and saved for the right one* (2 Cor. 6:14-17).
10. *Pray that they will learn to submit totally to God and actively resist Satan in all circumstances* (James 4:7).
11. *Pray that they will be single-hearted, willing to be sold out to Jesus Christ* (Rom. 12:1-2).

12. *Pray that they will be hedged in so they cannot find their way to wrong people or wrong places, and the wrong people cannot find their way to them* (Hos. 2:6).

There comes a time in our children's lives when we can do little more than pray for them and hope we've been good models and teachers for spiritual development. There will be times when we're disappointed with their choices, but there will also be times when we're pleasantly surprised.

In June 1995, I spoke to the Promise Keepers gathering in the Houston Astrodome. I've had the privilege of speaking at a number of those events over the last couple of years, and I always look forward to it. I often take Joel with me when I go. Those are awesome days, and many men's lives are changed as a result.

I was scheduled to be the second speaker on the second day of the Houston rally, which was a Saturday. I had spent some time early in the morning in prayer and preparation before I went to the stadium, but I wanted to be alone a little longer so I'd be ready when my time came. I slipped off to one of the private boxes in the stadium that had been set aside for the speakers. I listened and prayed, and as the current speaker closed, he asked everyone in the stadium to pray with someone. It was then that I wished I'd asked Joel Porter to come to the box with me. I thought about going to look for him, but I knew I didn't have time.

I prayed alone for about five minutes. Then I heard the door open behind me, and Joel Porter slipped in right beside me. "Dad," he said, "everyone's praying, so I wanted to pray with you."

I put my arm around him, and we spent a wonderful time together.

I've prayed with many great men of God in my life—James Dobson, Bill Hybels, E. Stanley Jones, Norman Vincent Peale, and others. But nothing compares with being able to pray with your own son during a special moment like that. Unasked, Joel Porter sought me out so the two of us could pray together.

Those minutes with him are what I cherish most from that Promise Keepers weekend. And they also give me great hope—hope that Joel and Elizabeth have received an adequate foundation in their spiritual development and will continue to grow closer to God as adults.

Breakthrough #10

Trust God—First, Last, and Always

The potential breakthrough for the parent . . .
proper perspective

The potential breakthrough for the child . . .
hope

Ever since Elizabeth was about four years old, she and I have had a tradition at Thanksgiving. We save the wishbone from the turkey and dry it on the windowsill in the kitchen. A few days later, when the bone is good and dry, each of us grabs an end, makes a wish, and pulls. Most of the time, Elizabeth wins. But I still remember the first time she didn't. We both pulled on the wishbone, and her end cracked, leaving me the bigger piece. She looked up at me and started to cry.

"Don't cry, Honey," I told her as I reached out and put my arm around her. "You don't need to be sad about not winning, because my wish was special. My wish was that *your* wish would come true."

She smiled and gave me a big hug. Everything was okay again.

I imagine that's the wish of every parent for his or her children—that their dreams would come true, that they would have the best of everything in life. But there are no guarantees. When we first become parents and our children are babies, we pray to God that He'll make us good parents and that *we* will make the right decisions. But as our children get older, especially when they're 11 or 12 years old, we begin to pray that *they* will make the right choices.

A HOPE FOR THE FUTURE

As parents, our goal should be to give our children roots and wings. In botany, roots do three things: They give plants stability by holding them into position, they draw nourishment from the soil, and they store food and water. For children, roots come from love for God, strong Christian values, a healthy self-image, the desire to learn, self-discipline, connection to the family, and belief in their potential. They give children stability, the ability to learn and grow, and reserves against storm or drought.

Wings give children the ability to fly—to make prudent choices, overcome obstacles, maintain a positive attitude, and choose a compatible, godly mate. To fly is to be able to reach their potential, to become the people God intended them to be.

HOW CAN I KNOW THEY WON'T STRAY?

Caring parents also know, however, that parenting has its limitations as well as its goals and potential. We can't guarantee a positive outcome in our children's lives. We can model good living. We can provide tools. But we can't make them use those tools. The choice is ultimately theirs, and as they become young adults, accountability shifts away from us and to them and their relationship with God.

About 10 years ago, I made a discovery while I was studying the kings of Judah and Israel in the Old Testament. I taught it to my congregation in a message called "Why Do Children Raised in a Christian Home Stray Away from God?" It has given comfort to many parents who couldn't understand why their best efforts met with poor results.

What I learned by studying four successive kings of Judah was that any kind of parent can produce any kind of child. Take a look at those four kings, beginning with Rehoboam, the son of Solomon:

- *Rehoboam was the father of Abijah.* A bad father begat a bad son (see 1 Kings 12:1-23 and 14:21-31).
- *Abijah was the father of Asa.* A bad father begat a good son (see 1 Kings 15:1-8).
- *Asa was the father of Jehoshaphat.* A good father begat a good son (see 1 Kings 22:41-50).
- *Jehoshaphat was the father of Jehoram.* A good father begat a bad son (see 2 Kings 8:16-24).

Just because a parent is good and godly doesn't mean his children will automatically follow in his footsteps. That was even true for the perfect parent—God. Adam and Eve still went the way of sin.

The bad news, then, is that even if you're a near-perfect parent, there's no *guarantee* your children will follow in your footsteps. But the good news is that if you *are* a good parent, the *likelihood* that your children will follow in your footsteps increases dramatically.

WHAT TO DO WHEN THE ROAD GETS BUMPY

No matter how skilled you are or how compliant your children have been, you will probably face a time when the road gets bumpy. What should you do then? The same things you do when the road is smooth—trust God, keep a positive perspective, and hang on for the ride. Here are 10 guidelines to help you do that:

1. Give Unconditional Love

Trust in God makes all things possible, but love makes all things worthwhile. Unconditional love and affirmation are a lifeline to children when they're going through tough times or self-doubt, helping them feel better about themselves. I'm reminded of a Peanuts cartoon I saw a few years ago. Charlie Brown receives a call from Peppermint Patty. She says, "Marcie and I are about to leave for camp, Chuck. We're going to be swimming instructors."

Then Marcie takes the phone and adds, "We just called to say good-bye, Charles. We are going to miss you. We love you."

As Charlie Brown hangs up the phone, his little sister, Sally, asks, "Who was that?"

With an enormous grin on his face, Charlie Brown answers, "I think it was a right number."

I know that when I was a child, I needed love most when I deserved it the least. And my parents provided it for me. When they disciplined me, they explained why they were doing it, and then about 30 minutes afterward, they would call me to them and hold me or hug me. They were very affirming, and the more difficult the time was for me, the more affirming they were.

As I got older, I always knew my parents were my best friends. That may sound corny, but it was true. I still remember my mother sitting me down at the kitchen table when I was 16 and talking with me about a teenage couple in our community who got into trouble. He was a senior in high school and she was a junior; I'll call them Fred and Jill.

"John, I want to talk to you about what happened with Fred and Jill," she said. "I don't know if you knew this, but Fred got Jill pregnant."

My face turned red. I knew who they were, but I didn't know them well. It was awkward to be discussing the subject with my mother.

"Their parents are just heartbroken," she said. "The children eloped last week because they wanted the baby to have its father's name, and they didn't want it to be born out of wedlock. But now it looks like Fred will have to drop out of school so he can get a job. His plan was to go to Ohio State and study to be a civil engineer, but I don't know that he'll ever be able to do that. Jill's hoping she can stay in school until the end of the year, but she won't be able to go back for her senior year now."

> # When I was a child, I needed love most when I deserved it the least.

She looked me in the eye and added, "John, I want you to know it's very important that you live a pure life. It's important to God, but it's also important to your future, especially if you're to be a preacher."

Then she reached out and placed her hand on my arm. "But let me tell you, Son," she continued, "that if you ever get into trouble—any kind of trouble—you come to us first, to me and your dad. We always want you to do right, but if you do wrong, don't run. We will always love you and help you through any storm."

Their love not only encouraged me to try to be good, but it also gave me a sense of belonging. I knew I would always be accepted by them, no matter what happened, and knowing that gave me tremendous freedom to achieve.

2. Parent in the Present

Parenting is difficult enough to do in the present without carrying around the baggage of the past. Maybe when you look back at your past as a parent, you see some mistakes. But before you begin to punish yourself for them, ask yourself this: At that time, did I do what I believed was best for my child? Your answer will almost always be yes, and if that's the case, move on. If the answer is no, learn from it, ask for forgiveness from God and your child (if appropriate), and move on.

Worrying about the future can be equally draining. Before you have a baby, people warn you that the child will keep you up all night. Then when you have the baby, they say, "Things are great now, but wait until he walks." When he's a toddler, they say, "He's cute now, but wait until he hits the terrible twos." Then they say, "Wait until he goes off to school . . . until he turns 12 . . . until he learns to drive . . . until he begins to date . . ." The list is endless.

The truth is that every stage of a child's development has its rewards as well as its downsides. There are always challenges to tackle and aspects to enjoy. Some of the stages you fear most may be peaceful. And the ones you expect to be relatively easy can be tough. That's why it only pays to focus on the present and take each day as it comes.

3. Lighten Up

I enjoy reading Shoe, the comic strip by Jeff MacNelly. I saw one not long ago in which Cosmo—the character everyone calls Perfessor—is talking to a pastor, who looks like a duck. The Perfessor asks, "Heard any good prayers lately, Padre?"

"As a matter of fact, yes I have, Cosmo," answers the pastor. "It's an old prayer that I find very useful these days:

> God grant me the serenity to accept the things I cannot change,
> the courage to change the things I *can* change, and the wisdom
> to know the difference."

The Perfessor responds, "Yes, I've heard that before somewhere. . . ."

"It comes in handy a lot," says the pastor. "Of course, I like to use the short version: Lighten up."

That's wise advice—especially for Margaret and me, because of our personalities. We're both cholerics who are used to taking charge and fixing things. We've always worked hard to correct things we thought were wrong with ourselves, but we discovered that trying to fix others is not a good idea. I found that out when people came to me for pastoral counseling. I was able to make them feel comfortable and secure with me, but I wanted to give them answers to their problems and steps to change themselves instead of letting them work through the problems.

I also found that the fix-it approach doesn't work well with kids. And sometimes the best thing to do is just back off and lighten up, especially when the issue is a matter of personal taste or temperament. That's why Margaret and I identified our top five priorities—to help us know when to take a stand and when to lighten up. Then when something like one of the kids' eating habits begins to bug us, we just stop and say to ourselves, "This too shall pass."

4. Remember You're Not the First Person to Travel This Road

Many problems you may be facing are typical and have been dealt with by other parents. Here are several problems common to most kids:

- Putting off homework
- Not wanting to do chores
- Forgetting to flush the toilet (small kids)
- Talking on the phone for long periods of time (teenagers)
- Being unable to save money
- Doing the bare minimum

If problems like these are getting you down, you have plenty of company. They are a regular part of being a parent, but they're temporary. Discipline children appropriately to help them become more mature, but be gentle. Overly harsh discipline for minor offenses is a motivation killer.

5. Don't Withhold Emotional Support

When the road gets bumpy, some parents withdraw from their kids emotionally. But during difficult times, children need emotional support. They can survive without their parents' money or advice, but they don't do well without love. And if they're not getting any at home, they may go looking for it in inappropriate ways.

Even when your kids have messed up badly or hurt your feelings, give them hugs and other signs of affirmation and affection. Show them you're glad they're yours. That assurance can carry them through the tough times. And it may help you, too.

6. Remind Yourself That You're Not Perfect, Either

Whenever you have the urge to pick at your children for little things they do, remind yourself that you're not perfect, either. Chances are, you've also recently forgotten to put your dirty clothes in the hamper, close the refrigerator tightly, turn off the lights, or eat your peas. Give them some grace. And don't forget that Scripture says we will be judged according to how we judge others (see Matt. 7:2).

7. Choose Your Battles Wisely

Our children will do many things while growing up that will drive us crazy. But how many of them really matter? Parents spend a lot of time picking at their children about things that won't matter in another year. Hair styles, clothing fads (as long as they're not indecent), and the beat of the music (as long as the lyrics are acceptable) are of little consequence.

I've been guilty of giving the wrong things attention, just as every other parent has. For example, Joel Porter cracks his knuckles, and it drives me crazy. But it's not something I should damage our relationship to change. We've all got to pick our battles. Thomas Jefferson offered this sage advice: "In matters of principle, stand like a rock; in matters of taste, swim with the current."

8. Try to Maintain a Long-Term Perspective

If you're facing problems, some of them may be genuine causes for concern. But others will work themselves out in time. When Elizabeth was in elementary school, for instance, she didn't like doing her homework. We had to continually encourage her and help her discipline herself to get it done. Margaret and I could have let this be a source of worry, but we didn't. We simply continued to help Elizabeth, and by the time she got to junior high school, it worked itself out. She's been an excellent student ever since.

Try to keep a positive, long-term perspective as you interact with your kids. Remember you're raising them for the long haul. Many strong-willed children who battle their parents as teenagers become close to them as adults. And who knows? Their quirks may be appealing to their future mates.

9. Get a New Definition of Parental Success

In breakthrough #3, I encouraged you to try to be a priority parent instead of a perfect one. I was asking you to change your view of what it means to be a successful parent. But that's really just half of the picture. Not only do you need to forget trying to be a perfect parent, but you also need to forget having perfect children. If you judge your success by whether your children turn out perfectly, you'll be setting yourself up to fail, because it will never happen.

I mentioned in breakthrough #4 that I came across a couple of my past definitions of success written in 1979 and 1992. But in 1994, I again rewrote my definition. My new one says, "Success is knowing that those closest to me love and respect me the most." You see, I finally realized that making my family my top priority and treating them well determined whether I was succeeding in life. When I treat them as I should, they respond to me positively.

I encourage you to get a new definition of success in the area of parenting. You can do no more than your best. You can control your actions, but ultimately, your children are in control of their own responses. So judge your parenting by these three criteria:

- *The quality of your love for your children*
- *The model you've been to them*
- *The appropriateness of your actions (and reactions) to them*

If you can continually score yourself high in these areas, you're doing fantastically well.

10. Trust God

Mother Teresa said, "I know God will not give me anything I can't handle. I just wish that He didn't trust me so much." When God gave us our children, He showed His trust in us, for He has given us lives whose value is beyond measure. Sometimes the responsibilities that come along with that trust seem overwhelming. Ironically, rather than turn to God, we often seem reluctant to give Him our trust, and we rely on ourselves instead.

Three turtles were going out on a summer afternoon for a country picnic. One carried a basket with the food, the second carried a jug of turtle-ade, and the third carried nothing. As they got close to their picnic site, they felt the first plop of raindrops on their shells.

"We can't have a picnic without an umbrella," said the first turtle. "One of us will have to go back for one." The first two turtles decided that the empty-handed turtle should be the one to go.

> When God gave us our children, He showed His trust in us, for He has given us lives whose value is beyond measure.

"I won't go," he said. "As soon as I leave, you'll eat all the food and drink all the turtle-ade. I won't get a thing."

"No, we won't," said the first.

"We'll wait for you," said the second, "no matter how long it takes!"

"No matter how long?" asked the third turtle.

"No matter how long!" said the other two.

The third turtle turned back, and the other two sat waiting. They waited an hour, two hours, four hours . . . a day, two days, a week. Two weeks went by, and finally the second turtle turned to the first and said, "Maybe we should go ahead and eat."

Just then they heard the voice of the third turtle call out from the bushes nearby, "If you do, I won't go!"

The truth is that only God is worth trusting. He is powerful, and we are powerless. We have no ability to change permanently the color of a single hair (see Matt. 5:36), and we can't add a single moment to our lives by worrying (see Matt. 6:27). We can't even say with certainty what will happen tomorrow (see James 4:14). But God has power over all things. He even knows when a sparrow falls to the ground (see Matt. 10:29).

PRAYER: THE TANGIBLE EXPRESSION OF TRUST

How does a parent put trust in God? Through prayer, the tangible expression of that trust. As my parents taught me, "When trouble comes, talk less, pray more."

Margaret and I have spent a lot of time praying with and for our children. Many times, I've come home late from work and passed by the kids' bedrooms, only to see Margaret praying over them as they slept. She has done that from the day they became ours. And often when things were difficult with the children, we stopped whatever we were doing and prayed with them.

Joel Porter always needed a lot of prayer as a child (and he continues to need it). I especially remember a time when we were on vacation at a camp in the woods of Georgia. Joel must have been about six or seven years old, and his behavior had been terrible. Early one morning, I left the mobile home we were staying in to get us all breakfast. I was gone maybe 20 minutes, but when I returned, Margaret was sitting on the steps of the trailer with Joel in her lap, and both of them were crying.

"What's happening, Babe?" I asked as soon as I saw them.

"Well," said Margaret, "I was talking with Joel about how he's been acting, and I felt I should pray with him about it. While we were praying, God came, and I think He did a work in both of us. Joel apologized for the way he's been, and I feel like a burden's been lifted from me."

For the rest of that trip, we saw a real turnaround in Joel's attitude and actions. Of course, we haven't always seen immediate results from our prayers. When you pray, you don't know what's going to happen; there's no limit to the number of ways God may answer. *Faith* in God helps you believe He can *take you out* of whatever's giving you trouble. *Trust* in God helps you believe He will take you by the hand and *walk you through* the trouble. But either way, it's good to know that whatever happens, you're in God's hands.

The writer of the book of Hebrews pointed out that God has said,

> "Never will I leave you;
>   Never will I forsake you."
> So we say with confidence,
>   "The Lord is my helper; I will not be afraid.
>   What can man do to me?" (13:5-6)

We can depend on God. He will never abandon us to the mercy of our circumstances. We can cast all our cares on Him because He cares for us, just as Peter told us (see 1 Pet. 5:7). C. H. Spurgeon remarked, "God is too good to be unkind. He is too wise to be confused. If I cannot trace His hands, I can always trust His heart."

Margaret and I are in a real "trust God, pray more" phase of our lives. Not long ago, we helped Elizabeth move into her dorm room at college. Between her car and ours, we were able to get all her things packed, and it didn't take too long to haul them up to her room. As we brought in the last box, Margaret started moving things around and decorating.

"I think the bed would look the best over against that wall," she said. "Then you could put the bookcase over there."

"Mom, I'll do it," Elizabeth said.

"And that picture would look really great over there," Margaret continued.

"Mom! I said I'll do it."

"Do you want me to help you hang the curtains?" Margaret asked.

Elizabeth looked dejected.

"Okay, okay, we'll go," Margaret said. "Can we at least pray with you first?"

Elizabeth agreed to that, and we spent about 20 minutes covering her in prayer and asking God to bless her time at college. As we left the dorm, I looked at Margaret and said, "We're done, Honey. Our parenting is over with Elizabeth. She's making her own decisions now. We're just going to have to trust God from here on out."

Slowly, we're learning to let go. It hasn't been easy. We spend a lot of time praying for Elizabeth, and we're trusting God more each day, just as I hope you will. But when I get really anxious, I think back to a lesson Elizabeth herself taught me a while ago.

I got a call from my brother, Larry, on an afternoon in May during a board meeting at INJOY, my leadership-equipping organization. Dad had suffered a heart attack. I was shocked, because Dad has always kept himself in great shape. He's not overweight, he has never smoked, he doesn't drink, and he exercises.

Dad did eventually recover, but back then, things looked bad. That night, Margaret and I decided I should fly to Orlando alone, catching the first plane out of San Diego. And in the meantime, the four of us prayed together for Dad. It was a tender time. My dad has always been my hero, and I love him so much. It looked as if he might slip away before I could get across country to see him. Our tears flowed as we prayed for him that evening.

I didn't sleep well that night, and I got up early the next morning. It was still dark when I went out to my car to head for the airport. As I settled into the driver's seat, I found a note taped to my steering wheel. It was from Elizabeth, and this is what it said:

DAD ~ Give everyone my love & tell grandpa especially that there is nothing to worry about, God is there — He knows All! :
I ♡ U Dad, please don't be Sad — He's in Gods arms.
                    Forever — E   ♡

And I thought, *Thanks, Elizabeth. I needed that. I* will *trust God.*

Afterword

One Last Breakthrough Thought

Margaret and I are grateful for all the help we've received over the years from the people in the churches where we've ministered, especially in the area of prayer. But as parents, there were many times when we wished someone would come alongside us and help us create a breakthrough in our children's lives. You've probably felt the same way. That's why I set out to write this book. My desire was to come alongside you and make a difference in your life and the lives of your children.

I recently received a letter from 10-year-old Kyle Beard, a boy whose mother is making a difference in his life. His letter contained two ribbons, a story, and the following message:

> Dear Dr. Maxwell,
> Hello. How are you? I know you are busy planning your annual Church Growth Conference in Toledo, Ohio. I listen to your tapes, and I know they help and interest my mom. So do the conferences. . . .
> Please read the attached story. My youth group is doing a project just like in the story. You are supposed to take the extra ribbon and give it to somebody that makes a difference in your life. The reason I am giving my ribbon to you is because you

have made a BIG influence on my Christian life. And ever since I listened to your tape about eagles, I have thought you are an eagle too. I know you are very busy, but if you could, find 5 minutes to write me back and tell me who you gave your ribbon to. Because in order to finish the project, I have to report back. I pray for you every night.

Your friend,
Kyle Beard

Here's the story Kyle included in the letter:

Who You Are Makes a Difference

A teacher in New York decided to honor each of her seniors in high school by telling them the difference they each made. Using a process developed by Helice Bridges of Del Mar, California, she called each student to the front of the class, one at a time. First she told them how the student made a difference to her and the class. Then she presented each of them with a blue ribbon imprinted with gold letters which read, "Who I Am Makes a Difference."

Afterwards the teacher decided to do a class project to see what kind of impact recognition would have on a community. She gave each of the students three more ribbons and instructed them to go out and spread this acknowledgment ceremony. Then they were to follow up on the results, see who honored whom, and report back to the class in about a week.

One of the boys in the class went to a junior executive in a nearby company and honored him for helping him with his career planning. He gave him a blue ribbon and put it on his shirt. Then he gave him two extra ribbons, and said, "We're doing a class project on recognition, and we'd like you to go out, find somebody to honor, give them a blue ribbon, then give them the extra blue ribbon so they can acknowledge a third person to keep this acknowledgment ceremony going. Then please report back to me and tell me what happened."

Later that day the junior executive went in to see his boss, who had been noted, by the way, as being kind of a grouchy fellow. He sat his boss down and he told him he deeply admired him for being a creative genius. The boss seemed very surprised. The junior executive asked him if he would accept the gift of the blue ribbon and would give him permission to put it on him. His surprised boss said, "Well sure."

The junior executive took the blue ribbon and placed it on his boss's jacket above his heart. As he gave him the last ribbon, he said, "Would you do me a favor? Would you take this extra ribbon and pass it on by honoring somebody else? The young boy who first gave me the ribbons is doing a project in school, and we want to keep this recognition ceremony going and find out how it affects people."

That night the boss came home to his 14-year-old son and sat him down. He said, "The most incredible thing happened to me today. I was in my office, and one of the junior executives came in and told me he admired me and gave me a blue ribbon for being a creative genius. Imagine. He thinks I'm a creative genius. Then he put this blue ribbon that says, 'Who I Am Makes a Difference,' on my jacket above my heart. He gave me an extra ribbon and asked me to find somebody else to honor. As I was driving home tonight, I started thinking about whom I would honor with this ribbon, and I thought of you. I want to honor you.

"My days are really hectic, and when I come home, I don't pay a lot of attention to you. Sometimes I scream at you for not getting good enough grades in school and for your bedroom being a mess, but somehow tonight, I just wanted to sit here and, well, just let you know that you do make a difference to me. Besides your mother, you are the most important person in my life. You're a great kid, and I love you."

The startled boy started to sob and sob, and he couldn't stop crying. His whole body shook. He looked up at his father and said, through his tears, "I was planning on committing suicide tomorrow, Dad, because I didn't think you loved me. Now I don't need to."[1]

The letter, ribbons, and story Kyle sent touched me—so much that I decided I needed to do something about it. When I received his letter, I was in the midst of preparing for the conference Kyle mentioned: the twentieth Church Growth Conference in Toledo. Each time INJOY does a church growth conference, we schedule it for all day on Friday and Saturday, and I preach an additional service on Friday night. The audience for that service is usually made up of more than 1,000 people, including several hundred pastors. I always ask God to send His Holy Spirit to renew the pastors' spirits and hearts for ministry. I also ask people who feel called to full-time Christian service to come forward and commit themselves to that intention. While preparing for that service, I read Kyle's letter and looked at the two ribbons he sent me, and I realized at that moment what I was going to do with the ribbon he wanted me to pass on.

Several weeks later, on the Friday night of the conference, the auditorium was packed. Nearly 3,000 people had registered for the weekend, and most of them came for the evening service. A little while before it began, I got together with my dad and a group of 25 prayer partners. As they laid their hands on me and prayed for me and the service, we sensed that God was going to come in a powerful way and change lives.

That night, I preached a message called "I Make a Difference" in which I talked about some of the little-known people in the Bible who made a big difference in the kingdom of God—people such as Rahab, the prostitute in Jericho who hid the Israelite spies. Because of her faithfulness, she became a part of the greatest family in Israel. She was the great-grandmother of King David—and the ancestor of Jesus. The Bible is filled with ordinary people who made a big difference in the lives of others.

I had also had thousands of ribbons made up that said, "I Make a Difference." I wanted there to be enough so that every person in the auditorium that night could have one to pin on himself and an additional one to pass on to someone else, just as that executive did for his 14-year-old son in the story. As I closed the service, I acknowledged some of the people who have made a great difference in my life, including my dad, who has been my model and mentor; my mother, who has always bathed me in prayer; and Margaret, who is the person most responsible for my success in life.

Then I told the story of 10-year-old Kyle Beard and how he was already making a difference, touching the lives of others in a positive way. I had asked him to come all the way from Liberty, Kentucky, to be there that night, and as I called him to walk up to the platform, everyone gave him a tearful standing ovation. Then I asked everyone in the auditorium to hold up his or her ribbon. I wanted Kyle to have a picture of the people he had touched because he passed along a ribbon to another person.

Hundreds of people came forward that night to commit themselves to full-time Christian service, and even more pastors recommitted themselves to their ministries. The Holy Spirit moved among the people in an incredible way and let them know they were, indeed, making a difference in people's lives.

Right now, I've got one ribbon left—and as a parent, I'd like to give it to you because *you* make a difference. The choices you make and the actions you take can change your children's lives. Maybe that will be the most significant breakthrough of all that comes from this book—the realization that you have the power to make such a difference. What you do to help your children has value, not only in their lives for the moment, but also for eternity. The people your children become will touch thousands of other lives.

Knowing you make a difference as a parent is your breakthrough. Now it's time to help your children experience theirs.

Notes

Introduction

1. Roger von Oech, *A Whack on the Side of the Head* (New York: Warner, 1983).
2. Ibid., p. 58.

Chapter 1

1. Jack Canfield and Mark Hansen, eds., *Chicken Soup for the Soul* (Deerfield Beach, Fla.: Health Communications, 1993), pp. 228-30.

Chapter 2

1. Florence Littauer, *Personality Plus* (Grand Rapids, Mich.: Revell, 1983), pp. 24-81.

Chapter 3

1. C. S. Lewis, *Mere Christianity* (New York: Macmillan, 1952), p. 86.

Chapter 4

1. Anthony Campolo, *The Power Delusion* (Wheaton, Ill: Victor Books), pp. 30-31.
2. Dorothy Law Nolte.
3. David Gergen, "The 50 Percent Catastrophe," *U.S. News & World Report*, October 2, 1995, p. 88.

Chapter 7

1. Lois Wyse, *Good Housekeeping*, April 1985.

Chapter 8

1. Natasha Tosefowitz, "I Have Arrived."
2. *Christianity Today*, August 27, 1976.
3. Stephen Covey, *The Seven Habits of Highly Effective People* (New York: Fireside, 1990), pp. 188-97.

Afterword

1. Helice Bridges, in Jack Canfield and Mark Hansen, eds., *Chicken Soup for the Soul* (Deerfield Beach, Fla.: Health Communications, 1993), pp. 19-21.

To find out more about John Maxwell's products and seminars for leadership development and personal growth, contact:

INJOY
1530 Jamacha Road, Suite D
El Cajon, CA 92019-3757
1-800-333-6506